DRIVE THE POINT HOME

DRIVE THE POINT HOME

200 stories for Speakers, Preachers and Teachers

Edited by

GRAHAM TWELFTREE

MONARCH
Crowborough

First published 1994

ISBN 1 85424 246 6

Produced by Bookprint Creative Services
P.O. Box 827, BN21 3YJ, England for
MONARCH PUBLICATIONS
Broadway House, The Broadway,
Crowborough, East Sussex, TN6 1HQ
Printed in Great Britain

To
Barbara

CONTENTS

PREFACE

I first heard preaching that faithfully and consistently communicated the good news when I was on the staff of All Souls Church of England, London. Especially from Michael Baughen, Richard Bewes, John Stott and other staff members, I saw the importance and power of the story of communication. I remain thankful for what I learnt from them. To this list I add the late David Watson whose use of stories and clear messages have been a great example to me.

I am grateful to David Girvan and Jeff Mountford, colleagues on the ministry team at Hope Valley Uniting Church in Adelaide. While I do not always appreciate or agree with their perceptive criticism each Monday at our staff meetings, they have greatly improved my talks and stories!

Many of these stories have made their way into my filing system with the help of Carol Webb, my long-suffering secretary, and the men and women on the front desk of our church offices. Thank you to these special people.

Once again I have been kindly served in this project by a number of librarians: Trevor Sweck and Ruth Strelan (Luther Seminary), Sue Goldsworthy (Tea Tree Gully City Council) and the staff of the State Library of South Australia. Thank you also to Graham Humphris (Adelaide), Robert Isles (Adelaide), Steve Silvester (Nottingham) and, once again, to Phil Muston (Darwin) for taking time to read and comment on a rough draft of what follows.

It has been a pleasure to work with Tony and Jane Collins of

Monarch. They are marvellously efficient as publishers. Also, a book like this is only possible through the generous permission of other authors, editors and publishers to use their stories. I gladly acknowledge my debt to them and hope readers find their way to their books and articles for yet more stories.

Unfortunately, I could not trace the origin of some stories and am sorry I cannot give due credit for them.

Each Saturday evening Barbara, my wife, looks over my talk or talks for the day ahead. For many years she has made comments that have helped rescue many an ailing talk. She has also found some of the following stories in her reading. In gratitude for her companionship in the privilege of proclaiming the best news of all – Jesus – I offer this book to her as a token of my loving appreciation.

Graham Twelftree
Adelaide, 1994

INTRODUCTION

Storytelling is as old as the camp fire. Storytelling is also powerful and life changing. We see this from the story and stories of Jesus and from our own experience when God uses a well-chosen story in one of our talks to help people hear his voice. However, I find the business of discovering good stories a relentless and difficult task. Also, like cooking a meal, the preparation and delivery of a talk is over in such a short time – and the stories have finished their life. Therefore, I hope this book helps some preachers in their search for good stories.

Why stories?

To provide interest, a good talk or sermon will contain jokes, quotations, personal and family stories, figures of speech and poems, for example. Above all, I am convinced of the importance of storytelling as an essential ingredient of a talk. Occasionally a sermon will consist simply of a few stories – or even just one story – with a very carefully honed introduction, application and conclusion. The Gospels indicate we have a good model for this in the preaching of Jesus. Stories are important to preachers for a number of reasons. For example:

- Stories attract and maintain interest, especially in difficult subjects.
- Stories help hearers identify with a message they may otherwise assume does not apply to them.

- Stories aid the memory in a world where there is much to remember.
- Stories enable the same points to be made many times in the same talk or over a series of talks without conveying the sense of repetition.
- Through engaging the emotions, stories can engage more of a person than a series of teaching points.
- Stories convince listeners of truth when they can imagine it in action.

What makes a good story?

Quite simply, a good story is one that helps communicate the speaker's message. What story will do this varies from culture to culture and audience to audience. Under the pressure of time and regular preparation, a story will rarely be found to have all the features we would wish. Nevertheless, while there are plenty of exceptions, a good story will generally have a number or many of these characteristics:

- An introduction that gives the hearers time to enter the scene or identify with the characters.
- Detail that gives integrity, fosters the imagination and aids the memory.
- Is factual rather than fictitious.
- Is specific rather than general.
- Has emotional content to engage the hearers.
- Is believable to help the audience believe the message.
- Tells of people rather than things.
- Tells of events rather than places.
- Is from the world of the hearers to help them identify with the message.
- Is no longer than necessary.
- Has no unnecessary details to divert attention.
- Does not betray family, personal or pastoral confidences.
- Does not assume too much from the hearers who may not, for example, read the same papers or watch the same television

programmes as the speaker.

- Is not told for its own sake, manipulating the message.
- Does not abuse or use people, especially the disadvantaged.
- Is told for the sake of the message and the hearers rather than the ego of the speaker.
- Has a carefully thought-out ending and application.

Some stories may have no function other than to attract interest and attention to the subject in general and need only be arresting, often through being humorous or topical.

Finding stories

Where does one find such stories? Some seasoned preachers suggest that daily vigilance will net stories from all aspects of life. However, most of us are not that creative. In any case, we would often want to be using stories that come from a wider sphere than our own experience.

As the bibliographical details attached to the stories in this book show, most of my stories come from reading. There are other sources as well.

- Popular Christian books.
- Church newspapers, for example: *The Baptist Times, The Church of England Newspaper, The Church Times.*
- Biographies of all kinds.
- Novels.
- Newspapers, especially weekend editions.
- Collections of sermon illustrations. For example: Robert Backhouse, *1500 Illustrations for Preaching and Teaching* (Marshall Pickering: London, 1991); Michael P. Green (ed.), *Illustrations for Biblical Preaching* (Baker: Grand Rapids, 1989); Paul E. Holdcroft, *Cyclopedia of Bible Illustrations* (Abingdon-Cokesbury: New York and Nashville, 1947); Water B. Knight, *Knight's Treasury of Illustrations* (Eerdmans: Grand Rapids, 1963); Paul Lee Tan, *Encyclopedia of 7700 Illustrations* (Bible Communications: Garland, Texas, 1979); Quilla Webb, *1001 Illustrations for*

Pulpit and Platform (Harper: New York and London, 1926).

- Journals, for example: *Alpha, Christianity Today, Decision, The Expository Times, Leadership, New Day, On Being.*
- Tapes, for example: 'The Pastor's Update' from Charles E. Fuller Institute of Evangelism.
- Weekly and monthly news magazines, for example: *The Bulletin, Life, Newsweek, Psychology Today, Time, Who?*
- Women's magazines.
- Teenage magazines.
- *Reader's Digest.*
- Devotional material, for example: *Every Day With Jesus*, Scripture Union Bible-reading notes, *The Upper Room.*
- Mission society publications and journals, for example: *East Asian Millions* (Overseas Missionary Fellowship: Epping, New South Wales); *Go* (Interserve: Box Hill, Victoria); *The Sower* (The Bible Society in Australia: Canberra).
- Other preachers' sermons.
- Church history, for example: J. Stevenson (ed.), *WA New Eusebius* (SPCK: London, 1992); J. Stevenson (ed.) *Creeds, Councils and Controversies* (SPCK: London, 1966).
- Theological reading.
- Sermon illustration periodicals, eg. *Pulpit Resource.*
- Books on preaching, for example, Ivor Bailey, *Prate, Prattle or Preach* (JBCE: Melbourne, 1987); Bill Hybels (et al.), *Mastering Contemporary Preaching* (Multnomah: Portland, 1989).
- Radio and television news, documentaries, current affairs, educational and talk-back programmes.
- Movies and videos.
- The theatre.
- Personal and family stories – always used with prior discussion and permission!

It would be impossible to subscribe to all the journals and magazines that might yield good stories. The local city and county council as well as university and theological libraries will need to be frequently visited.

Using the stories

Some of the stories that follow are exactly as I have used them, others are as they are filed or found in the original source. However, most stories will need to be carefully reintroduced and reworked to suit the preacher's character and style as well as audience. Because stories can illustrate many different points and themes, most of the stories that follow do not have an application or a conclusion. Even the conclusions which are occasionally found below will need to be redrawn and the story reapplied for the particular audience and theme.

A few of the longer stories which follow (for example, number 168), could yield more than one shorter story. Some stories, especially the more humorous ones (see index), will work best in the early stages of the talk; more emotive stories towards the end. Some of the stories will need to be used with care! Stories such as numbers 42, 123, 195 and 200 will not suit all audiences. In all cases, a careful record should be kept of when and where stories have been used.

Most stories can be used to illustrate a number of different themes. Therefore, the possible conclusions or implications have rarely been drawn out in the stories. Nevertheless, as well as the subject or theme-heading given to each story, at the end of each entry is a series of suggested topics in which the story could also be used. The indexes at the end of this volume will also help in tracking down a story for a particular theme.

To help the biblical preacher, an extensive list of passages often occurs at the end of each entry. Where a passage is paralleled in more than one Gospel, generally only Mark has been cited for the triple tradition and Luke for Q passages. All the passages mentioned are cited in the index to biblical passages.

The Stories

1: Abortion

To the Editor: in the annual report of the committee reporting on abortions notified in South Australia, the committee chairman, Professor L.W. Cox, stated that, although abortion is a procedure associated with a known risk, in 96% of the abortions performed in 1982 there were no complications.

I had an abortion in South Australia in 1982 and, seeing that I did not suffer from haemorrhage, sepsis or damage to the uterus (the complications about which committee was concerned), I presume that I was included among the 96% of women who suffered no complications following the procedure. I would like to tell a different story.

Although I was ambivalent about my pregnancy (it was unplanned), I did want to keep my baby. My husband, however, was very hostile to the idea. I had severe hyperemesis, and because I was so ill I could not cope with my husband's anger towards my children and myself. At the time, to agree to his demands for an abortion seemed the only solution to the problem.

For the first four months after the abortion, I cried more or less all day and all night. I would wake myself up sobbing in my sleep fitfully, would have terrible nightmares about dying children. During the day I would do things like going around the house rocking an imaginary baby in my arms, or scattering rose petals over the garden. I was haunted by the fact that my baby had had no funeral, and I would play the same piece of sad music over and over again obsessively, each time mentally burying my baby. It was spring, and the sight and scent of flowers seemed to mingle with, and heighten, my grief. I had no one to share my grief with, and nothing to focus it on. I felt physically exhausted all the time.

Within a month of the abortion, my hair started turning grey. I almost lost my part-time job because I cried so often at work. When I drove the car I was frequently blinded by tears, and had several minor accidents, any one of which could have been serious. I often had thoughts of killing myself and my children.

Then came the terrible anger which ate away at me for months, and finally the time of deep depression when I just lay on the bed all day. I was absent-minded, lethargic and withdrawn.

Today seventeen months after the abortion, the grief, the anger and depression, although diminished, are still there. I still find it difficult to cope with the sight of babies or pregnant women. I have several sexual and identity problems, my relationship with my surviving children has been damaged, my marriage is in ruins, and I am under the care of a psychiatrist.

Please, let all doctors be aware, if they are not already aware, the abortion is not 'just a ten minute procedure' but can have very serious and long-lasting psychological consequences.

(Name withheld by request.)

Themes: Family, Grief, Marriage ethics, Suicide.

Scriptures: Exodus 20:13; Deuteronomy 5:17; Job 31:15; Psalms 22:9–10; 71:6; 119:73; 139; Ecclesiastes 11:5; Isaiah 49:1,5; Jeremiah 1:5; Matthew 5:4; 2 Corinthians 1:3–4.

2: *Abortion*

I was having a lot of difficulty with my feelings about late abortions – and all the pain that's there so much of the time after the baby is moving. So one day, in order to arrive at the measure of clarity, I went into the room where they keep the foetuses before burning them. They were next to the garbage cans in paper buckets, like the take-home chicken kind. I looked inside the bucket in front of me. There was a small naked person in there, floating in a bloody liquid. He was purple with bruises and his face had the agonising tautness of one forced to die too soon. I then took off the lids of all the other buckets and with a pair of forceps lifted each foetus out by an arm or a leg, leaving, as I returned them, an additional bruise on their acid-soaked bodies. Finally I lifted out a very large foetus and read the label – mother's name: C. Atkins; doctor's name: Saul Marcus; sex of the item: male; time of gestation: twenty-four weeks (six months). I remembered Miss Atkins. She was seventeen, a very pretty blonde girl. So this was Master Atkins – to be burned tomorrow – for the sake of his mother.

Themes: Christians at work, Human life, Medical ethics, Promiscuity.

Scriptures: Exodus 20:13; Job 31:15; Psalms 22:9–10; 71:6; 139; Ecclesiastes 11:5; Isaiah 49:1,5; Jeremiah 1:5.

3: *Abortion*

The story is told of a woman who went to a doctor in Bonn, Germany, to ask for an abortion. The father had a sexually transmitted disease. They already had four children. The oldest one was blind. The second had died. The third was deaf and dumb. The fourth child, as well as the mother, had TB. The doctor held out little hope of a healthy fifth child.

If you were the doctor would you have agreed to an abortion? An abortion would certainly ease a great deal of suffering for the mother and the family.

If you had agreed to that abortion you would have killed Beethoven.

Themes: Christians at work, Hope, Human life, Medical ethics, Sexually-transmitted diseases.

Scriptures: Exodus 20:13; Job 31:15; Psalm 22:9, 10; 71:6; 119:73; 139; Ecclesiastes 11:5; Isaiah 49:1, 5; Jeremiah 1:5; 1 Peter 1:13.

4: Adoption

During a heated argument, an Arab struck and killed another man. Knowing the inflexible custom of his people, the young Arab ran across the desert until he came to the big sprawling tent of the tribal chief. The young fellow confessed his guilt and asked for protection. The old chief put his hand on one of the guy ropes of his tent, swore by Allah, and accepted the murderer into his tent of refuge. He was now safe.

The next day, others came looking for the fugitive. However, the chief would not let the pursuers take the young man.

'But, do you know whom he has killed?' they asked.

'I have not the slightest idea.'

'He has killed your only son!'

The chief's heart and mind began to fill with confusion. Then the old sheik looked at the young man he had accepted. He said,

'You have killed my son. But I am going to make you my son, and you will inherit everything I possess.'

News of that particular story reached a nearby Christian hospital. Some of the patients who had heard about Jesus recognised that just as the sheik had offered his son in death for the freedom of a stranger, so God has offered his Son's death in our place.

Themes: Acceptance, Easter, Forgiveness, Sacrifice.

Scriptures: Mark 11:25; Romans 5:8; 8:14–17, 23, 32; 9:4; Galatians 4:5–7; Ephesians 1:5.

5: Adoption

Until he faced his painful past, our new son would never know peace – or joy.

The first time I saw the little boy who was to be my son, he was huddled on a brown vinyl couch in a psychologist's office. Pale, with dark stubbly hair and nail-bitten fingers, he sat near a silent couple in their mid-forties, his adoptive parents, I assumed. It was Wednesday 15 June, 1987. Michael was four years old. My husband, Terry, and I weren't supposed to see him, but we did as we hurried by. Abandoned as a toddler by his natural mother, Michael was about to be told that he was being given away again. We heard later that when the psychologist told him he'd have to leave his mummy and daddy and get a new mummy and daddy, he began to tremble convulsively. Then he soiled his pants.

Terry and I decided to adopt a child after thirteen years of marriage – and three children of our own. We enrolled in classes offered by the welfare authorities and listened as Sheryl, one of the adoption workers, told us about the children available through the public agency. We heard horrifying stories, stories of toddlers locked in cupboards and choked unconscious by drunken parents, and looked at photographs that left us shaken and nauseated.

I went home from the first few meetings in tears. I'd rather not know about this stuff, I thought with a shudder. Can I really deal with a child who's been through things like that? But at the end of the course we had submitted an adoption application.

The wait lasted exactly nine months. Our family was on holiday when Sheryl called. 'I think I've found a child for you,' she said. 'His name is Michael.'

Then she filled in the tragic details. Michael's mother, a drug-user, had repeatedly tried to give him away. He was twenty-two months old, still in nappies, when she abandoned him with a broken arm and two black eyes at a fast food restuarant.

Michael spent over a year in foster care before being placed with a family. But for Michael it led to another rejection.

'He's a typical four year old,' Sheryl told us. 'But his adoptive parents have never had children, they don't seem to know what to expect from a little boy. They want him out of their home by Friday.'

She paused. 'I know this is short notice, but there's something very special about this particular child. Would you consider taking him?'

Terry was on an extension nearby. I looked over at him; he returned my gaze, then nodded.

We hurried home. The day after we saw the frightened little boy in the psychologist's office, Sheryl arranged a get-aquainted meeting. We were prepared for Michael to be tearful and depressed, but he seemed surprisingly cheerful.

'Are you my new mum and dad?' he asked brightly. 'I'm supposed to move into your house tomorrow.' He giggled nervously as we told him about his new brother and sisters, but I noticed that he avoided our eyes.

On Friday morning, Terry and I went to pick up Michael at his adoptive home, an impressive house with flawless furnishings and immaculate white carpets. We carried Michael's meagre possessions out to our car, and then it was time for him to say a final goodbye to his parents. His smile remained fixed as his mother gave him an indifferent pat. When his father swept him up in a bear hug, however, his small chin began to quiver. He raced to our car, shouting, 'Let's go!'

On the way home, Michael laughed and chattered animatedly. Only once, when he thought we couldn't hear him, did he express what he was feeling. 'I wanted to tell my grandma goodbye,' he whispered. Terry and I exchanged worried glances: this small stranger, our *son*, had a lot to deal with.

When we pulled into our driveway, Michael looked taken aback: our modest brick home was a sharp contrast to the one he had just left. The differences became even more marked when we went in to be mobbed by three excited children and a dog; of necessity, our furniture and carpets were the sturdier, stain-resistant variety.

Michael smiled shyly as we introduced him to Lisa – eleven, Rachel – seven and Steven – five. 'A lot of kids live here,' he observed. He asked where they had all lived 'before this family' and seemed confused to hear that they'd always been with us.

Over the next few days, Terry and I concentrated on getting to know our new son. We discovered that his unhealthy pallor came from having rarely been allowed outdoors. He worried constantly about getting his clothes dirty. 'My other mummy used to get real mad,' he finally confided. 'She took away all my socks because I kept messing them up, and then I could only wear socks on a Sunday.'

Terry was disgusted. He took Michael for a long walk around the neighbourhood – and back through a muddy field. When they got back Michael was filthy but giggling.

We expected the first few weeks to be difficult for Michael. Instead, he seemed almost casual in his acceptance of us. He played happily with the other children and called us Mummy and Daddy with apparent ease. We were pleased – until our neighbours let us know he was calling them Mummy and Daddy as well. The words evidently held no special meaning for him.

Dark Emotions. Our first hint of real trouble came one day in late June. During breakfast Michael spilled cereal on his clothes and I told him to go and change. When he didn't return, I went to his room. He was standing motionless by his dripping bedpost, watching a puddle of urine spread across the floor.

'Why did you do that?' I asked gently. He looked up with an empty expression, then dropped his eyes and stood silent.

Had he thought I was punishing him? I could only guess. But the incident was a startling reminder that our child was struggling with issues – abuse, abandonment, rejection – that no four year old was equipped to face.

June turned to July. At night Michael often awoke screaming, but during the day he seemed happy, remarkably even-tempered, and never angry or upset. His face had taken on a healthy glow, and he seemed to enjoy a boyish camaraderie with Steven. Then something happened that left us deeply shaken.

I walked into the kitchen one afternoon to find Michael standing alone, a look of despair on his face, and a sharp butcher's knife pressed to his stomach.

'Michael!' I shouted. 'Put it down!' I lunged forward and snatched the knife, then collapsed into a nearby chair.

Hands trembling, I drew him onto my lap. 'Honey, what were you doing?'

His answer was chilling: 'I was wondering what it would be like to go to heaven.'

That night Terry and I stayed up late talking – and praying. 'What made me think we could change the life of an abused child?' I asked my husband. 'Was it a mistake to think about adopting?'

'No,' Terry said. 'No. We can make a difference, we *are* making a difference.'

Terry and I had come to rely strongly on our instincts as parents; we felt that, with patience, we could help Michael express the dark emotions that were troubling him. After checking with the psychologist, I decided to take a simple approach.

The next morning, I called Michael into my room. 'Let's play a game,' I suggested. 'Let's try pretending we're very, very sad.'

'That's a funny game,' he observed, becoming immediately restive. He had, after all, been probed by psychologists and case workers much of his young life.

We sat cross-legged on the bed, taking turns frowning into a hand mirror. After a few minutes I said 'Now let's tell some things that make us sad. I'll start: It makes me sad when people say mean things to each other. How about you?'

He nodded 'It makes me sad when – ' Abruptly, he stopped and jumped off the bed. 'I don't want to play this game,' he muttered.

I knelt beside him on the carpet. 'Honey, I know this is hard, but I want you to try. Can you just whisper something in my ear?'

After a moment he leaned close; I felt his warm breath. 'It makes me sad when people say they don't like me any more. And... and go away.' As he spoke, his small body began to shake.

'It's all right,' I said, wrapping him in my arms, '*I'll* always love you.' He hugged me back fiercely, but his anguished blue eyes were tearless.

As the summer progressed, Terry and I worked closely with Michael. We noticed he smiled when he was actually angry. So we began to stop him whenever he was disguising his feelings.

One day, Michael stormed in from the boys' bedroom: 'It's not fair! Steven took all my racing cars!'

We placated him and sent him back to tell Steven to share. 'I never thought I'd be so glad to hear a kid yell,' said Terry, smiling.

By the end of August, Michael was able to express his anger and seemed more confident of his place in our family. But he continued to conceal his distress about the traumatic events that had led him to our home. In the ten weeks he'd been with us, he had never cried.

'I think he's afraid of opening that last locked door,' I told Terry one day as we sat drinking coffee.

'Maybe we need to force the issue,' Terry suggested. 'We can't let him go on like this; it's not healthy.'

The opportunity arose unexpectedly one hot afternoon. Michael was playing contentedly with some blocks. 'It was fun one time when my other daddy helped me build a tower,' he said. 'We threw things at it until we knocked it down.'

I smiled from across the room. 'I'll bet you had a lot of nice times with your "old" daddy didn't you?'

His silence made me look up. Although he quickly averted his face, I could see his chin quivering.

'Let's talk about your "old" father,' I said.

He tried to squirm away, but I pulled him close, then cupped his face in my hands, making him look at me square in the eyes. 'Those feelings won't go away until you talk about them,' I said softly. 'Can't you do that?'

I sensed the deep struggle within him as he glanced wildly around the room, looking for escape. In his desperate expression I suddenly saw the infant whose cries had gone unanswered, the tot whose outstretched arms were twisted and broken. I saw the trusting three year old who'd been told he could stay 'forever' in an adoptive home and was then rejected. I saw hurt, betrayal, anger – and, beneath it all, a deep desire to be loved. Tears streamed down my face.

'Michael?' He looked numbly into my eyes. I knew the time had come to topple the last barrier he'd erected around himself.

'When you were a baby,' I began unsteadily, 'your mother used to hit you. Once she hit you so hard she broke your arm. Then she left you somewhere all alone. How did that make you feel?'

He was barely audible. 'Sad.'

'And then the mummy and daddy who were supposed to adopt you decided they didn't want you after all.' The words hurt to say, and I swallowed before plunging on: 'How did that make you feel?'

'Sad,' Michael answered.

I nodded tearfully. 'Then you went to a foster home, and just when you were feeling happy with your new mummy and daddy, you had to leave them too. How did that make you feel?'

Raw anguish filled his eyes. He stared mutely.

'It's OK,' I said, almost pleading. 'You don't have to be afraid of those feelings any more. I'm going to be your Mummy for ever.'

His eyes remained locked on mine for a moment; then, with a shuddering wail, he collapsed into my arms and began to sob with deep, wrenching gasps. I held him tight and wept with him, feeling his hot tears soaking my shirt.

He cried for three days. It was as if a dam had burst. He would remember the church outfit his mother hadn't let him pack, the fishing trip his "old" daddy had never taken him on and the fishing rod – the symbol of that promise – he had to leave behind. Then he would wail again. On and on, between hugs and talk, he cried. I cried with him through each physical enactment of past pain. Slowly we began to leave it all behind.

On 23 November 1987, Michael legally became part of our family. He is now a bright and mischievous eight year old who hopes to be 'either a doctor or a postman' when he grows up. And he's doing well at school.

Michael's breakthrough didn't solve all his problems. He's still greatly distressed by any loss, and grieves deeply when teachers or friends move away. But I have begun to measure his progress by his reactions to these leave-takings.

Terry travels frequently on business and, at first, each time he left, Michael would be distraught. So I established a simple ritual that helps assure him: in his life with us every parting anticipates a return.

Michael carries his dad's bag to the old van Terry uses as his 'airport bus'. Then we hug, all of us. We say goodbye, I love you, hurry back soon. Michael and I stand outside the house and wave until the van is out of sight.

'Daddy's just going away on business, isn't he?' Michael asks me. 'But he'll be back with us soon, right Mummy?'

'Yes,' I say, the words 'with us' warming my heart. Yes, my son. I encircle him with my arm, and draw him close.

Themes: Acceptance, Easter, Love – transforms, Parenting, Sacrifice.

Scriptures: Luke 10:27; Romans 5:8; 8:14–17, 23, 32, 9:4; 1 Corinthians 13; Galatians 4:5, 6, 7; Ephesians 1:5.

Note: Names have been changed to protect the identities of the individuals involved.

6: Adoption

During the Korean War a guerrilla fighter murdered the son of a Christian minister in order to undermine the Christian influence in the village. Later he was captured and put on trial. The grief-stricken father gave evidence against the man.

But then, to everyone's amazement, the minister pleaded – not for justice but for the life of the murderer of his son. The minister offered to adopt the murderer. In the confusions of war-time it was permitted.

As a consequence, the guerrilla-fighter became a Christian. The minister had turned his quite justifiable verdict of 'guilty' into a verdict of 'accepted'. This stunning act is only a reflection of what God has already done for each of us.

Themes: Accepted, Easter, Forgiveness, Sacrifice.

Scriptures: Mark 11:25; Romans 5:8; 8:14–17, 23, 32, 9:4; Galatians 4:5–7; Ephesians 1:5.

7: *Adoption – Ancient Roman*

It was a serious step to take a child out of one *patria potestas* (father's power) and to put him into another. It was, however, not uncommon, for children were often adopted to ensure that some family should not become extinct but should continue to exist. The ritual of adoption must have been very impressive. It was carried out by a symbolic sale in which copper and scales were used. Twice the real father sold his son, and twice he symbolically bought him back; finally he sold his lad a third time, and at the third sale he did not buy him back. After this the adopting father had to go to the *praetor*, one of the principal Roman magistrates, and plead the case for the adoption, and only after all this had been gone through was the adoption complete. But when the adoption was complete it was complete indeed. The person who had been adopted had all the rights of a legitimate son in his new family, and completely lost all rights in his old family. In the eyes of the law he was a new person. So new was he that all debts and obligations connected with his previous family were cancelled out and abolished as if they had never existed.

Themes: Acceptance, Easter, Forgiveness, Sacrifice.

Scriptures: Mark 11:25; Romans 5:8; 8:14–17, 23, 32, 9:4; 1 Corinthians 6:20; 7:23; Galatians 4:5–7; Ephesians 1:5–6.

8: *Adventure*

About 350 years ago a shipload of travellers from Europe landed on the northern coast of America. The first year they established a town site. The next year they elected a town government. The third year the town government planned to build a road five miles westward into the wilderness. In the fourth year the people tried to impeach their town government because they thought it was a waste of public funds to build a road five miles westward into a wilderness. Who needed to go there anyway?

Here were people who once had the vision to see three thousand miles across an ocean and overcome great hardships to get there but had now lost their vision.

Themes: Faith, Certainty, Creativity, Leadership, Risk, Vision.

Scriptures: Matthew 28:19; Mark 11:22–24; Luke 7:1–10; Acts 1:8; 13:1–3.

9: *Anger*

It is said that when Leonardo da Vinci was working on his painting 'The Last Supper', he became angry with someone. Losing his temper, he lashed the man with bitter words and threats. Returning to his canvas, he attempted to work on the face of Jesus, but was unable to do so. He was so upset he could not compose himself for this painstaking work. Finally, he put down his tools and sought out the man and asked for his forgiveness. The man accepted his apology and Leonardo was able to return to his workshop and finish painting the face of Jesus.

Themes: Character, Communion, Confession, Eucharist, Forgiveness, Humility, Last Supper, Reconciliation, Tongue.

Scriptures: Genesis 4:5, 23–24; 27:43–45; 1 Samuel 18:8–9; 19:9–10; 20:30–31; Job 18:4; Psalms 4:4; 37:8; Proverbs 14:29; 29:22; 16:14; 20:21; Ecclesiastes 10:4; Matthew 5:22–24; Mark 11:25; Luke 18:9–14; Galatians 5:20; Ephesians 4:26, 31; 6:4; Philippians 2:3–11; Colossians 3:8; 1 Timothy 2:8; Titus 1:7; James 1:19–20.

10: Beauty

Cher invests big in the body beautiful. London – Oscar-winning film star Cher has invested about $55,000 in the past decade in her quest for the body beautiful, says *Paris Match* magazine.

'The physical retouches are the secret of her magical youth and legendary silhouette at the age of forty-one', says *Paris Match*.

Cher says that in 1981 she spent $3,000 on removing traces of acne from her face. Another $4,200 was invested on having the size of her navel reduced and two ribs were removed to give her torso that slender boyish look.

Since her nose was 'gigantic', Cher had that done too – at a cost of $6,000.

Her jaw had been rounded off and cheekbones made more prominent. She has also had her teeth capped ($4,200), a bust operation in 1969 ($7,500), followed by another round in this department in 1979 and 1983, her buttocks rounded ($7,500) and her thighs reduced ($6,000).

Themes: The Body, Materialism, Self-esteem, Vanity.

Scriptures: Romans 12:3–6; 1 Corinthians 12:12–27; Ephesians 4:12-16; Colossians 1:18; James 2:15; 3:6.

11: Bible

When Anatoly Rudenko was a student at Moscow University in his late teens, he was an atheist and a communist. While he was studying economics at university, he began to ask the big questions in life. He wondered if there was some superior power over us – a God. In a certain situation he asked God for help. God answered his prayer. Anatoly said that he then wanted to find out more about this God. He heard that there was such a book as a Bible and he became very keen to read it.

Just to get one Bible he made a seventy-two kilometre journey from Moscow to Zagorsk. He found a monk in a Russian Orthodox Church and pleaded with him for a Bible. It was 1976 and the Bibles were scarce. Eventually, the monk agreed to give him one of these rare and valuable books. But Anatoly had his bag stolen at university and his Bible was gone. He so much wanted to read the Bible that he made yet another trip to pester the monk for another copy.

Themes: Doubt, God, Inspiration, Perseverance, Russia, Students.

Scriptures: Psalms 14:1; 53:1; Matthew 5:18; 8:26; 14:28–31; John 10:35; 2 Timothy 3:16–17; Hebrews 11; 2 Peter 1:20–21.

12: *Bible*

In 1787 Captain Bligh took the ship *The Bounty*, on a voyage around the world to collect bread-fruit trees. When he reached Tahiti in the central southern Pacific he found a veritable paradise. Soon every sailor had a girlfriend. There was quite a deal of grumbling when Bligh announced that after a few months in this heaven on earth they were leaving.

Not many days out of Tahiti, Bligh woke up to find himself looking down the barrel of a gun. Bligh and eighteen officers were put in a small boat without maps. Fletcher Christian and eight mutineers took the ship back to Tahiti and the pretty ladies. There they convinced not eight but twelve girls to go with them. They set off again for fear of being caught. They had no plans and came across Pitcairn Island. It was another island paradise. They took as much of their things as possible onto the island and then set fire to the ship.

What looked like paradise turned out to be ten years of hell. One of the sailors used a copper kettle to make a distillery. They drank the 'fire-water' made from the tree roots. The men spent days, weeks and months on end 'plastered' by the spirits. Some of the men went mad and became like animals. They fought among themselves. One jumped off a cliff. After several years there were only two men left. Edward Young and Alexander Smith. Young was old, ill and asthmatic.

One night the women seized the guns and barricaded themselves and their eighteen children off from the men. Neither the women nor the children would go near the two men.

One day, Young went to the ship's chest and, at the bottom among the papers, he found a book. It was a leather-bound, old, mildewed and worm-eaten Bible. He had not read for years and Smith could not read at all. So Young taught him. The two men, frightened, disillusioned and utter wrecks, together read the Bible. They started at Genesis. They saw from the Old Testament that God was holy and that they were sinful. They did their best to pray.

The little children were the first to come back to the men. They noticed a change in the men. Then the children brought the women. They sat and listened to them read. During this time Young died. Then Smith came to the New Testament. Something important happened to him as he read the story of Jesus in the Bible.

'I had been working like a mole for years,' he said 'and suddenly it was as if the doors flew wide open, and I saw the light, and I met God in Jesus Christ, and the burden of my sin rolled away, and I found new life in Christ.'

Eighteen years after the mutiny on *The Bounty*, a ship from Boston came across the island of Pitcairn and the captain went ashore. He found a community of people who were godly. They had a love and peace about them that he had never seen before. When the captain got back to the United States he reported that in all his travels he had never seen or met a people who were so good, gracious or so loving. They had been changed by the message of the Bible.

Themes: Conversion, God – holy, Holiness, Human nature, Jesus – Light, Light, Love – of others, Paradise, Prayer.

Scriptures: Genesis 1:3–4; 1 Samuel 2:2; Job 10:22; Psalms 14:1; 27:1; 53:1; Isaiah 9:2; Habakkuk 1:13; Matthew 5:18; Luke 10:27; 16:8; John 3:19–21; 8:12; 9:5; 10:35; 12:36, 46; 13:1, 34–35; 17:11; Acts 4:30; Romans 7:14–25; 8:29; 12:2; 1 Corinthians 13; 2 Corinthians 3:18; 4:6; 6:14; Galatians 5:19; Ephesians 5:8; Colossians 3:10; 1 Thessalonians 5:5; 2 Timothy 3:16–17; 1 Peter 1:13-16; 2:9; 2 Peter 1:20–21.

13: *Bible*

Mr Yang, a builder of Shen Yang Province in north-east China, once owned more than one Bible. However, during the cultural revolution he had to stand by despairingly as his Bibles were taken from him and burnt.

Later he was delighted to hear some good news. A man not far away had been able to hide his Bible successfully. The same man had, for some time, been asking Mr Yang to take his son on as an apprentice.

With a twinkle in his eye, MrYang said, ' At the time I was a builder. I did not normally take on apprentices, but when I heard that man had a Bible, I agreed to take the boy as an apprentice if he would let me borrow the Bible.'

When he got the Bible, Mr Yang began to copy it by hand. But he was tired at night after his long hard days of labouring, so he asked his seventeen year old daughter to help him.

'That was a good move,' said Mr Yang, 'because after she had copied out some of the Scriptures she became a Christian, and is now studying the Bible in seminary.'

They persisted with their laborious task for two long years and completed the four Gospels, Revelation, the Psalms and Proverbs. The manuscripts were then circulated among the members of Mr Yang's village who had been attending church in his house. In this way church members were able to study and obey God's word, despite the terrible upheaval in their country.

Theme: China, Church growth, Church planting, Conversion, Persecution.

Scriptures: Psalms 1:2; 14:1; 53:1; 119; Matthew 5:18; John 10:35; 2 Timothy 3:16-17; 2 Peter 1:20-21.

14: Bible

Marion was studying English at university. In the second term she had to write an essay on a particular modern writer. She found his work boring, to say the least. She could not get into his novels or short stories and the deadline for her essay loomed closer and closer with little good work done.

Glad to have the chance to get away from study, she went with some of her friends from her year to a party at their tutor's home. Among the clatter of glasses and the thump of loud music she enjoyed the conversation. During the evening her tutor introduced her to a very good-looking man in his early thirties. He seemed to know a lot about literature and was very interesting. Marion could feel herself falling for him.

During the conversation, to her surprise, Marion discovered him to be the modern writer who was the subject of her essay. That night she went home and in the small hours started to read page after page of his work and found it exciting and worthwhile.

Themes: Bible – inspiration, God – knowing, Students, Study, University.

Scriptures: Psalms 14:1; 53:1; Matthew 5:18; John 10:35; 2 Timothy 3:16–17; 2 Peter 1:20–21.

15: Bible – Influence of

A Russian teenager, living in Paris around 1930, was aggressively anti-Christian and hated everything to do with God. After listening unwillingly to a talk by a priest, he decided to read a Gospel to check whether the priest's picture of

Christianity – which the young man found repulsive – was supported by the Gospel account. Not to waste time unnecessarily, he chose Mark, the shortest Gospel. Before he reached the third chapter, he suddenly became aware that on the other side of his desk stood the risen Jesus. His hostility crumbled and he became a disciple of Christ. Today he is Metropolitan Anthony, the Russian Orthodox Archbishop in London.

Themes: Atheism, Conversion, Visions.

Scriptures: Psalms 14:1; 53:1; Matthew 5:18; John 10:35; 2 Timothy 3:16–17; 2 Peter 1:20–21.

16: Christmas

Jim Prince, a tall, strapping 18-year-old loved to play football.

On his first day in the front-line trenches at Ypres, Belgium, in 1914, he passed some bread to a fellow-soldier who, rising to take it, stuck his head above the parapet. A German sniper's bullet killed the soldier instantly.

Some 250,000 Allied and German troops were killed or wounded in the month-long Battle of Ypres that autumn. The First World War became bogged down in deadlock. The opposing sides were hidden in cold, water-logged trenches extending from the English Channel to the Swiss border.

Graham Williams, aged 21, of the London Rifle Brigade, peered over the parapet towards the German lines. Normally, no man's land was filled with shadowy figures darting here and there: some reconnoitring, others trying to retrieve dead and wounded. Tonight, however, an eerie stillness hung in the crystal-clear air.

He saw a light in the east, just above the German trenches and too low to be a star. Williams was surprised tht no one shot at it. He saw another light. And another. Suddenly, lights were all along the enemy trenches as far as the eye could see.

Then, from a German trench no more than 50 metres away, a chorus of the richest baritones Williams had ever heard began singing '*Stille Nacht, Heilige Nacht*.' ('Silent night, holy night'). When the carol was finished, William's regiment cheered – and sang 'The First Noel.' The mutual serenading went on for an hour interspersed with cries of 'Come over and see us, Tommy!' and 'No, Jerry *you* come over here!' But neither side moved.

In Jim Prince's part of the front, a German sang '*Stille Nacht*' standing on top of a parapet – a perfect target. Prince's regiment responded with 'While shepherds watched their flocks by night'. Then amazingly, the German started walking towards the British, followed by half a dozen other Germans, all unarmed, with hands in pockets.

For a moment, it looked as if they were going to surrender, but the British started climbing out of their trenches, too. Prince was among them. Five metres from a German, he stopped. Here was one of the enemy he'd been shooting at. The German said simply: 'I am a Saxon. You are an Anglo-Saxon. Why do we fight?'

Recalling this extraordinary moment many years later, Prince admitted: 'I still don't know the answer.'

Peace now swept through no-man's land. Soldiers from both sides shook hands, laughed, insisted they bore no malice against each other and vowed to continue the truce throughout the coming day.

Christmas Day dawned cold, clear, sparkling – and peaceful. No man's land was soon filled with thousands of soldiers from both sides, walking arm in arm and taking photographs. Several football matches were staged, mostly knockabout affairs with a tin can for a ball and caps for goalposts. One Scot managed to produce a real football. Meticulous sportsmanship was the rule. 'If a man got knocked down, the other side helped him up,' said one participant.

Some men cut buttons off their tunics as Christmas gifts. A German officer handed over the spiked helmet he wore with dress uniform, and was given a tin of bully beef in return. Soldiers with skills contributed what they could. One Englishman, a former hairdresser, gave haircuts to docile Germans kneeling on the ground. A German who was a professional juggler so enthralled his audience that it wasn't hard to imagine him as the Pied Piper of Hamelin, leading the British army behind the lines and into a prison camp.

It was also an opportunity for a solemn task in no man's land. Soldiers of both armies dug graves side by side. Then the chaplain, aided by a German divinity student, conducted a burial service.

By sunset, there had been almost no firing along the entire front for 24 hours, and as a result, the birds came back. None had been seen on the battlefield in months, but now sparrows were everywhere.

The 1914 Christmas truce continued in a few sectors of the front until New Year's Day or even later. 'We *had* to have it last that long,' one German explained in a letter home. 'We wanted to see how the pictures they took turned out.'

The general agreement was that when one side had to break the truce, they would fire a *feu de joie* into the air to give the enemy time to get back to their trenches. In Jim Prince's sector, the *feu de joie* came on December 29, and the men scrambled back to their trenches to cries of 'Go back, Tommy!' or 'Go back, Jerry!' Only minutes later, firing resumed in earnest.

For Prince, the football-lover who was to lose a leg several months later, the most wonderful Christmas he had ever experienced was over. And until he died in 1981 at the age of 85, he could never hear 'Silent night, holy night' without tears streaming down his cheeks.

Themes: Joy, Peace, War.

Scriptures: Psalm 34:14; Isaiah 9:6; Luke 2:14; 10:20; John 14:1–4; 15:11; 16:33; Romans 5:1–5; 1 Corinthians 7:15; Ephesians 1:9; Philippians 4:6–7; 1 Thessalonians 5:13; 2 Timothy 2:22; 1 Peter 3:11.

17: Commitment

In the second century, a Christian businessman went to Tertullian and explained his problem. He had been contracted to provide materials for a pagan temple. The man ended his story by saying to Tertullian, 'What can I do? I must live!'

Tertullian replied 'Must you?'

Themes: Business, Christians at work, Compromise, Faith, Integrity, Materialism, Risk, Trust.

Scriptures: Psalm 37:3–5; Proverbs 3:5–6; Matthew 6:24–34; Mark 8:34–38; 11:22–24; Luke 7:1–10.

18: Commitment

A Christian in Nepal, from a village near the city of Kathmandu, had spent much time in jail for his change to Christianity.

After he had been released, a series of unfortunate events happened in his family, culminating in the death of a daughter in a fall from a tree. (In Nepal women cut leaves for animal fodder.) The local villagers threatened that if he gave his daughter a Christian burial he would be charged with the murder of his daughter!

The dear man went ahead with the Christian funeral service so that, when this story was reported, he was returned to jail to await trial for murder.

Themes: Discipleship – cost of, Faithfulness, Persecution.

Scriptures: Matthew 25:14–30; Mark 8:34–38; 11:22–24; Luke 7:1–10; Acts 4:1–22; 6:8; 8:3; 9:23–25; 14:5–6; 16:19–24; 21:30–36; 1 Corinthians 4:11–13; 13:3; 2 Corinthians 6:4–5; 11:23–28; 1 Thessalonians 2:9; 2 Thessalonians 3:8.

19: Commitment

Two hundred years ago, Thomas Boston became the minister of a church in Ettrick in Scotland. He found that Christians were living such lax lives, and their relationships with each other were so poor, that he refused to allow the Lord's Supper to be held for the first three years. At the first communion service he held, he gave out only fifty-six tokens to people whom he considered were living lives honouring to the death of Christ. Then for twenty-two years, he encouraged the Christians to live lives honouring to the death of Christ. As they did, their lives together became attractive and something that others wanted to join.

At the end of his ministry, twenty-four years later, he presided over his last communion in that town. There were three days of preaching and preparation. On the day before, he and his elders gave out 777 tokens to persons to come to the Lord's Supper.

Themes: Communion, Confession, Discipline, Eucharist, Evangelism, Faithfulness, Holiness, Last Supper, Leadership.

Scriptures: Matthew 25:14–30; Mark 11:22–24; 14:12–25; Luke 7:1–10; Acts 2:43; Romans 12:2; 1 Corinthians 11:17–34; 1 Thessalonians 5:6; 1 Peter 1:13–16.

20: Cross

Christ did not carry the whole cross, only the cross-piece or *patibulum*. This was made of cypress wood and weighed 75–125 lbs, about as heavy as a bag of cement. Being forced to carry this the 700 yards of narrow, winding streets from Pilate's praetorium to the execution ground at Golgotha was an extra torture for an already flogged – almost flayed – man.

The nails securing Christ's arms to the cross were driven through the wrists, not his palms. The palms could not withstand the weight of the body: the hands would tear through longways. Instead, the eight-inch nails were driven precisely into the space between the wristbones. These were dislocated, but not shattered.

An important nerve, the median, crosses the wristjoint. The square-edged nails almost always came into contact with the nerve, stretching it over the sharp sides of the nail like the strings over the bridge of a musical instrument. This caused such severe cramp in the thumb that it bent across the palm so violently that the thumbnail embedded itself in the flesh.

The next step was to hoist the victim and slot the crosspiece onto the verticle stem or *stipes*. The knees were bent until the sole of one foot could be pressed flat against the *stipes* and an eight-inch nail was driven through it, precisely in the middle between the second and third metatarsal bones. As soon as the nail emerged through the sole, the other leg was bent into position so that the same nail could be hammered through the second foot and into the wood. The victim was then left to hang from the three nails.

A body suspended by the wrists will sag downwards, pulled by gravity. This produces enormous tension in the muscles of the arms, shoulders and chest wall. The ribs are drawn upwards so that the chest is fixed in position as if the victim has just drawn a large breath – but cannot breathe out. The condemned man begins to stifle.

The severely strained arms, shoulders and chest muscles develop agonising cramp. The metabolic rate is raised, but the oxygen supply is reduced.

One result is the production of large amounts of lactic acid in the bloodstream, leading to what is known as 'metabolic acidosis', often seen in athletes driven to exhaustion and severe cramp. This is aggravated by the difficulty in breathing and in ridding the body of carbon dioxide, leading to 'respiratory acidosis'. Unrelieved, the victim finally dies of suffocation. This can occur within half an hour.

So swift a death did not satisfy the Romans. This is why they nailed the feet too. The condemned man could buy time by pushing himself up on the nails in his feet, stretching his legs and so raising the body to relieve the chest and arms. This allowed him to breathe better – for a while. But perching with the full weight of the body on a square nail driven through the middle bones of the feet brings intolerable pain. The victim soon lets his knees sag until once more he is hanging from the wrist, the median nerves again strung over the nail shafts. The cycle is repeated to the limit of endurance.

There were endless 'refinements'. The torture could be prolonged by using ropes instead of nails, reducing the pain but lengthening the struggle. A sort of seat could be fixed to the vertical stem of the cross, allowing further temporary respite. When this was used, the death throes could be made to spin out for two or even three days.

The executioners could shorten the ordeal too, smashing the legs, thus making it impossible for the dying man to push himself up to breathe.

Excessive sweating brought severe thirst. Blood loss and oedema caused by flogging reduced the circulation volume, blood pressure fell and the heart pounded faster. The severely acidotic condition of the blood, combined with the excessive loss of salt through sweat, was barely compatible with life. The heart began to fail and the lungs filled with fluid. The beginning of the death rattle croaked in each failing, painful breath as his heart began to give out.

Themes: Christ's suffering, Crucifixion, Easter, Execution, Jesus – his death, Suffering.

Scriptures: Mark 10:45; 15:21–37; Philippians 3:10; Hebrews 5:8; 13:12; 1 Peter 2:21; 3:18; 4:1.

21: *Church – problems*

A minister in London once said that he sometimes dreams of the perfect church.

The worship is perfect, the problems non-existent, the personnel *vibrant*. Barry Tone is a superb director of music, ably assisted by his associate, Benny Dicktus and a superband, the Magnifi-Cats. Neil Down is the director of pastoring, Percy Vere co-ordinates the evangelism, and exercising a strict rule over the training is Ben Dover. Sally Forth maintains the missionary interest, Benny Factor handles the money, while Dina Mite is a church co-ordinator and Sue Prem is rector's assistant – the Rector being a firm, no-nonsense individual by the name of Dick Tate.

However, he recognises that the reality of the church life is very different. A more nightmarish, yet often more true-to-life team, he said, might include Mark Time, Peter Out, Molly Coddel and the gossip Di Vulge.

Themes: Church problems, Following, Gifts of the Spirit, Music, Leadership, Pastoral care.

Scriptures: Romans 12:4–8; 1 Corinthians 12:12–31; Ephesians 4:11.

22: *Church – relevance*

One cannot forget that when men were manning the barricades in Moscow in 1917 and preparing to fire the first shots of a world revolution, church dignitaries were holding a meeting in the same city for the specific purpose of deciding what colour of robes were to be worn at a certain ecclesiastical festival.

Themes: Church mission, Church politics, Evangelism.

Scriptures: Mark 6:7–13; Luke 4:16–21; 9:1–6; 10:1–20.

23: *Discouragement*

In Zundert, Holland in 1853 a Lutheran pastor became the proud father of a baby boy. At sixteen the boy went to work for a firm of art dealers in the Hague. A few years later he took the opportunity to travel to England. There he fell in love with his landlady's daughter, but she rejected him. In his grief he turned to Christ. He began helping a Methodist minister in Turnham Green and Petersham. The conviction grew that he should become a full-time evangelist, and in his mid-twenties he returned to Holland. He soon found great success in preaching to the poor, dressed like a peasant and living in their company. He washed their clothes, cared for their sick, consoled their dying and he led them to Christ.

However, the church leaders of the day would have nothing to do with him and forced him to give up his ministry. Eventually he gave up following Christ. He went back to the world of art and tried his hand in painting. His name was Vincent van Gogh. If he had not been discouraged, van Gogh might have been able to express his commitment to Christ through his art.

Themes: Church – leaders, Encouragement, Love.

Scriptures: Psalms 23; 42:6–11; 55:22; Matthew 5:11–12; Luke 10:27; Romans 8:28; 14:19; 1 Corinthians 10:23; 13; 2 Corinthians 4:8–18; Ephesians 4:29; Philippians 4:4–7; 1 Thessalonians 5:11.

24: *Easter*

During the days of communism in Russia, according to a report I read, Easter sunrise services were replaced by sunrise communist rallies.

One such meeting was particularly large; 10,000 people were present. At the close of the meeting, the communist leader asked if there was anything anybody wanted to say. Nobody moved. Eventually, a teenaged boy came forward. As he stepped onto the platform and approached the podium, the leader warned the boy, 'You must tell only the truth. If you do not you will be shot.' The truth the communist leader required was a denial of Christ and applause for communism.

All eyes were fixed on the lad as he stood there about to speak. He was flanked by soldiers, rifles pointed at his head. For several brief moments he remained silent. Then, standing tall and taking a deep breath, he called into the microphone, 'Christ is risen!'

At the same time that the crack of rifles rang out, 10,000 voices filled the morning air: 'Christ has risen indeed!'

Themes: Communism, Courage, Persecution, Resurrection, Suffering.

Scriptures: Psalm 27:14; Matthew 28:1–10; Mark 8:34–38; 16:6; Luke 24:1–11; John 20:1–8; Acts 7:54–8:1; 1 Corinthians 15:1–58.

25: *Encouragement*

Professor Margaret Kuhn is a research scientist working on the migratory habits of wild geese. These birds fly thousands of kilometres across whole continents in their migratory flights. Professor Kuhn discovered some interesting facts that enable the birds to fly such long distances. One factor is that they rotate the leaders. Another is that they always choose the leaders – the up-front birds – from the ones who can handle turbulence. And there is the important point. The other birds just honk along! This honking is not the agony of being out of breath. The birds behind the leader birds are honking encouragement to their leaders.

Themes: Barnabas, Humour, Leadership.

Scriptures: Acts 11:22–26; 15:41; Romans 14:19; 1 Corinthians 10:23; Ephesians 4:29; 1 Thessalonians 5:11.

26: *Endurance*

Shun Fujimoto is a gymnast and physical education teacher from Japan. He was twenty-six when he competed in the 1976 Summer Olympics team gymnastics in Montreal. *Newsweek* carried this story:

> During his floor excercise, Fujimoto fractured his right leg. But with the Japanese in contention for a team gold medal, he refused to give up. Fitted with a plastic cast from hip to toe, he somehow competed in the ring exercises – and achieved the highest score of his life. He finished with a triple somersault and twist that doomed him to excruciating pain when he landed. But he executed it flawlessly and fearlessly and maintained his balance long enough to clinch the gold for his team – before his leg crumpled grotesquely beneath him.
>
> 'It is beyond my comprehension,' said an Olympic doctor who treated Fujimoto, 'how he could land without collapsing in screams. What a man.'
>
> 'Yes, the pain shot through me like a knife,' said Fujimoto. 'It brought tears to my eyes. But now I have a gold medal, and the pain is gone.'

Themes: Courage, Future glory, Pain, Perseverance, Self–control, Sport, Suffering.

Scriptures: Psalm 27:14; Luke 21:9–19; Romans 8:8; 1 Corinthians 9:24; 1 Timothy 2:9, 15; 3:2; 2 Timothy 1:7; 2:3; Titus 1:8; 2:1–6, 12; Hebrews 12:1.

27: *Euthanasia*

One Sunday in London we took a long time to get home from church. The traffic had been halted by an anti–abortion rally in Hyde Park near where we lived. John, one of the members of staff, was at the rally. He said that one of the most moving speeches was made by Alison Davis. She described herself as 'a happy spina bifida adult'. And she spoke from a wheelchair. She also said, 'I can think of few concepts more terrifying than saying that certain people are better off dead, and may therefore be killed *for their own good.*'

Themes: Disablement, Grief, Medical ethics, Murder.

Scriptures: Exodus 20:13; Deuteronomy 5:17; 30:19; Job 31:15; Matthew 5:21–22.

28: *Evangelism*

On Saturday morning, 21 April 1855, Edward Kimball decided to speak to one of his eighteen-year-old Sunday school pupils about becoming a Christian. The young man worked in a shoe factory and Kimball was, at first, unsure about calling on him during working hours. But he decided to go in and see him. He found him in the back of the factory wrapping up shoes in paper and stacking them on the shelves. Kimball went up to the lad and put his hand on the lad's shoulder. There were tears in Kimball's eyes as he encouraged him to respond to Christ's love.

Kimball said that the young man was ready for the conversation so that, there and then, he gave himself and his life to Christ.

The lad decided that he would gather some derelict young people together. He asked a leading church to send over some Sunday school teachers to tell the gathering about Christ. By his own efforts and hard work of inviting folk, he gathered 1,200 young people to come each week and hear the stories of Jesus.

His name was D.L. Moody, the great American evangelist of the last century, who eventually held crusades around the world. Because an ordinary Christian told a lad about Jesus, thousands ended up knowing about him.

Themes: D.L. Moody, Obedience, Witnessing.

Scriptures: Mark 6:7–13; Luke 10:1–20; John 1:35–51; 4:1–42; 14:15–24; Acts 1:8; 5:29; 10:1–48; 1 Peter 3:15.

29: Evangelism

Scene: 6pm on the London Underground Bakerloo Line. It is a hot Friday evening. The carriage is crowded with tired commuters. Those lucky enough to be sitting are doing their best not to catch the eyes of those standing.

I noticed a tall impressive young man entering the train. As the doors closed and the train moved out towards Piccadilly Circus, he cleared his throat and started to speak.

'My friends, please listen to me for a few minutes. I am here to tell you Jesus loves you. If you do not follow Jesus you will go to hell. But Jesus loves you and asks you to follow him.'

As he went on people studiously read their evening papers and fidgeted – anything but look at him. But he continued. He had clearly worked out the timing of his script which ended just as the train pulled into Oxford Circus. 'Thank you my friends for listening. Remember, Jesus loves you, and I love you too.'

He left the carriage without looking back. But the passengers had been surprised out of their Friday evening apathy. Some laughed. Quite a few applauded. And then the people began to talk to one another. Who said that speaking on the London Underground isn't an appropriate model for evangelism?

Themes: Courage, Preaching, Witnessing.

Scriptures: Psalm 27:14; Mark 6:7–13; Luke 10:1–20; John 1:35–51; 4:1–42; Acts 1:8; 8:26–40; 17:22–34; 1 Peter 3:15.

30: *Evangelism*

An evangelist in Central America was at a university trying to win students to Christ. They showed him a great deal of hostility. After a particular meeting, a girl, who was working on her doctorate, came to him and said, 'I don't believe any of that hogwash.'

He said, 'Well, I don't think I agree, but do you mind if I pray for you?'

She said, 'No one ever prayed for me before. I don't guess it will do any harm.'

He bowed his head, but she looked straight ahead and was defiant when he started to pray. As he prayed for the conversion of that girl, the tears began to flow down his cheeks. When he opened his eyes, she was broken up with tears and said, 'No one in my whole life has loved me enough to shed a tear for me.'

They sat on a bench and she accepted the Lord as her Saviour.

Themes: Compassion, Love, Opposition, Personal evangelism, Witnessing.

Scriptures: Mark 6:7–13; Luke 10:1–20, 27; John 1:35–51; 4:1–42; Acts 1:8; 8:26–40; 17:22–34; 1 Corinthians 1:18–29; 13; 1 Peter 3:15.

31: Evangelism

In Algeria a woman Christian worker, who spoke Arabic well, would often engage a certain man in conversation about the divinity of Jesus, his mission to save us and our need to submit to him.

One particular day, after a lively dialogue, the woman was unable to respond further to his arguments. Smiling, he seemed pleased to think that no one would persuade him to accept Christ. Then quietly, the woman began to cry.

Concerned, he asked 'Aren't you well? What is the matter?'

'Nothing,' she replied. 'It's because of your reluctance to recognise God's love for you.'

He was deeply moved by her reaction. After a moment of silence he said 'A religion which moves someone to tears over someone else's spiritual welfare must be authentic.' He was converted.

Themes: Compassion, Empathy, Love, Personal evangelism, Witnessing.

Scriptures: Mark 6:7–13; Luke 10:1–20, 27; John 1:35–51; 4:1–42; Acts 1:8; 8:26–40; 17:22–34; 1 Corinthians 1:18–29; 13; 1 Peter 3:15.

32: Evangelism – urgency

Hudson Taylor was one of the greatest missionaries of modern times. He spent much of his life in China, introducing people to Jesus.

Once he was travelling by a small boat from Shanghai to Ningpo. In his cabin, Taylor was preparing to go ashore. He was startled by a sudden splash and a cry. Springing quickly up on deck, he discovered that Peter, a Chinese friend, had fallen overboard. Taylor begged some men with a drag net to pull in the drowning man. They refused because it was not, as they said, convenient. He offered them $5 to stop fishing and try to save Peter. They said they would do it for no less than $30. Taylor only had $14 – which they eventually accepted.

But it was too late. Even though Peter was brought on deck with the first sweep of the net, all attempts to revive him failed. Taylor's comment on this sad event is interesting.

'We condemn those fishermen. We say they were guilty of a man's death because they could easily have saved him and did not do it. But what of the millions whom we leave to perish, and that eternally?'

Themes: Missionary work, Missionaries, Love for others, Life – its price, Salvation, Tragedy.

Scriptures: Psalms 91; 118:5–6; Matthew 9:37–10:15; 28:16–20; Mark 6:7–13; Luke 8:22–25; 10:27; Acts 1:8; 1 Corinthians 13.

33: Evil – the problem of evil

Elie Wiesel was a survivor of Auschwitz. 'One day,' he says, 'when we came back from work, we saw three gallows in the assembly place. There were SS all around us, and machine guns were trained. There were three victims, including a child, in chains. All eyes were on the child. He was lividly pale, almost calm, biting his lips. The three victims mounted the chairs together. Their necks were placed at the same moment within the nooses.

'Long live liberty!' cried the two adults.

But the child was silent.

'Where is God? Where is he?' someone behind me asked.

At a sign from the head of the camp, the three chairs tipped over. Total silence throughout the camp. On the horizon the sun was setting.

'Bare your heads!' yelled the head of the camp. His voice was raucous. We were weeping.

'Cover your heads!'

Then the march past began. The two adults were no longer alive. Their tongues hung swollen, blue-tinged. But the third rope was still moving; being so light, the child was still alive.

For more than half an hour he stayed there struggling between life and death, dying in slow agony under our eyes. And we had to look him full in the face. He was still alive when I passed in front of him. His tongue was still red, his eyes were not yet glazed.

Behind me, I heard the same man asking,

'Where is God now?'

And I heard a voice within me answer him,

'Where is he? Here he is – he is hanging here on this gallows.'

Themes: Cross, Crucifixion, Holocaust, Suffering.

Scriptures: Job; Mark 15:21–39; Romans 5:6–11; 1 Corinthians 15:3; 2 Corinthians 5:14; 1 Peter 3:18.

34: Evil – the problem of evil

The Salvation Army preacher, Commander Booth-Tucker, was in Chicago trying to lead a sceptic to Christ. With a cold, glittering eye and a sarcastic voice he said, 'It is all very well. You mean well, but I lost my faith in God when my wife was taken out of my home. It is all very well, but if that beautiful woman at your side lay dead and cold by you, how would you believe in God?'

Within one month Mrs Booth-Tucker was killed in a terrible train accident. The Commander went back to Chicago, and in the hearing of a large crowd of people said, 'Here in the midst of the crowd, standing by the side of my dead wife as I take her to burial, I want to say that I still believe in God, and love him, and know him.'

Themes: Faith, God – belief in him, God – love for him, Grief, Testing, Tragedy.

Scriptures: Job; Psalms 91; 118:5–6; Matthew 5:4; Mark 11:22–24; Luke 7:1–10; 8:22–25; 10:27; 1 Corinthians 13; 2 Corinthians 1:3–11; James 1:2.

35: Evil – the problem of evil

In his later years, the famous French painter, Renoir, apparently suffered badly from arthritis. His friend Matisse once asked him, 'Why do you keep painting when you are in such pain?'

Renoir replied, 'The pain passes, but the beauty remains!'

Themes: God – faithful, Perseverance, Suffering, Testing.

Scriptures: Job; Matthew 5;11–12; James 1:2; 1 Peter 1:6; 4:14; 5:10.

36: *Exorcism*

A thirty-two-year-old, twice-married woman was brought in because of falling spells which had been treated with all kinds of anticonvulsant medication. She was examined on the neurosurgical service, and after all examinations – including EEG, brain scan and pneumoencephalogram – were negative she was transferred to the psychiatric service. Her mental-status examination was unremarkable and all the staff commented that she seemed normal until she had her first 'spell'.

While standing at the door of the day-room she was violently thrown to the floor, severely bruising her arm. She was picked up and carried to her room, resisting violently all the while. When the author arrived, eight people were restraining her as she thrashed about on the bed. *Her facial expression was one of anger and hate.* Sedation resulted in sleep. During the ensuing weeks the patient was treated psycotherapeutically and it was learned that there had been considerable turmoil in her childhood home, but because she was pretty she had been spoiled. She married the type of individual described by Jackson Smith as the first husband of a hysterical female. She was a 'high-liver' and after her separation and divorce, she was threatened with rejection by her parents. She remarried and her second husband was a nice but unexciting man. She continued to associate with her 'high-living' friends. When her husband demanded that she give up her friends and her parties, she started having her 'spells'.

The usual psychotherapeutic treatment for hysteria, including interviews under sodium amytol, only aggravated her spells. Seclusion in the closed section brought her assaultative and combative behaviour to an end but she would have spells in which she became mute, especially when religious matters were discussed. More dramatically, when the names of Jesus or Christ were mentioned she would immediately go into a trance. On one occasion while in a coma, in desperation, a demon was exorcised and her spells ceased. She subsequently accepted Christ as her Saviour and has been well ever since.

Themes: Deliverance, Demonic, Demons, Evil spirits, God – his power, Healing, Jesus – his name, Medicine, Psychiatry, Spirits, Suffering.

Scriptures: Psalm 34; Mark 1:21–28; 5:1–20; 7:24–30; 9:14–29; Acts 16:16–18; 19:11–20.

37: *Faith*

A small plane was flying near Cleveland, Ohio.

'Cleveland Centre, this is 346 Alpha Charley. I'm at 10,500. I'm in the clouds...not instrument rated. Would like radar vectors. Out.'

'Six Alpha Charley, Cleveland. Roger. Understand you are not instrument rated. Set transponder code 4582 for radar identification. What is your heading now, sir?'

'Six Alpha Charley is heading 250 degrees. Say again code. It's rough. I'm getting disorientated...I can't see the ground!'

'Six Alpha Charley, Cleveland. Set code 4582. Concentrate on your altitude indicator, sir. Keep wings level and reduce power to start slow descent. We have you on radar contact.'

'I'm losing control ... losing it ... turning ... I'm going to spin! ... I'm spinning! ... which way! Help! Help!'

'Six Alpha Charley, release your controls, sir! Look at your altitude indicator. Opposite rudder, opposite rudder....'

'Help! Help! I can't stop....'

'Six Alpha Charley, Six Alpha Charley, do you read?'

(Silence)

'Radar contact is lost.'

The above was based on a recorded conversation between a control tower and a small plane which crashed, killing the pilot. The investigation of this crash revealed that nothing was wrong with the flight instruments in N346 Alpha Charley.

Themes: Fear, God – in control, Guidance, Trust.

Scriptures: Exodus 13:21–22; Deuteronomy 31:6, 8; Psalms 23:4; 25:9; 32:8; 34:4; 37:3–5; 48:14; 66:12; 138:7; Proverbs 3:5–6; Isaiah 43:2; Daniel 3:25, 28; Matthew 10:28; Mark 11:22–24; Luke 7:1–10; 12:5; John 20:24–29; 2 Timothy 1:7; Hebrews 11:1–3; 13:5–6.

38: *Faith*

In 1859 Charles Blondin, the French acrobat, walked across a tightrope suspended across Niagara Falls.

One day, thousands watched him as he pushed a bag of cement in a wheelbarrow along the wire, fifty metres above the raging waters. There was a great cheer when he reached the other side.

Then, Blondin challenged a nearby reporter: 'Do you believe I can do anything on a tightrope?'

'Oh yes, Mr Blondin,' said the reporter. 'After what I've seen today, I believe it. You can do anything.' However, the reporter melted into the crowd when he was invited to put his trust to the test and get into the wheelbarrow.

But, there was a person there who did trust Blondin with his life. He got into the wheelbarrow and was pushed across the wire. As Blondin made his way high above the falls, people quickly placed bets on the outcome. It looked like any other easy conquest. But, when they were half way across the 500 metre journey of trust, a man with a heavy bet against

Blondin's success, crept across and cut one of the guy ropes.

Suddenly, the tightrope pitched crazily back and forth. Blondin fought for his balance, only seconds away from death. For, when the rim of the wheelbarrow came off the wire, they could both be pitched into the churning water. Blondin spoke, cutting through the terror of his passenger. 'Stand up!' he ordered. 'Stand up and grab my shoulders.'

The man sat there paralysed.

'Let go and stand up! Let go of the wheelbarrow! Do it or die!'

Somehow the man managed to stand up and step out of the swaying wheelbarrow.

'Your arms ... put them around my neck! Now, your legs ... round my waist!' said Blondin.

Again the man obeyed, clinging to Blondin. The wheelbarrow fell, disappearing into the frothy turmoil far below. The aerialist stood there, using all his years of experience and every trained muscle to stay on the wire until the pitching subsided a little. Then, inch by inch, he made his way across, carrying the man like a child. Finally, he deposited him safely on the other side.

Themes: Courage, Fear, God – in control, Guidance, Jealousy, Trust.

Scriptures: 2 Kings 18:5, 19–25; Psalms 2:12; 7:1; 9:10; 13:4–5; 16:1; 25:2, 20; 27:14; 31:1; 32:8; 34:4; 37:3–5; 38:15–16; 44:4–8; 56; 62; 73:28; 84:8–12; 91; 94:16–23; 112; 115:9–11; 146:3; Proverbs 3:5– 6, 21–27; 4:10–19; 11:28; 28:26; 29:25; Isaiah 12:2; 26:3–4; 36:1–10; 63:10–14; Jeremiah 17:7–8; Matthew 10:28; Mark 11:22–24; Luke 7:1–10; 12:5; John 20:24–29; 1 Timothy 4:10; 5:5; 2 Timothy 1:7; Hebrews 11:1–3; 13:5–6.

39: *Faithfulness*

During the conflict with the Koreans, communist soldiers moved into a peaceful village. One day the soldiers made all the people gather in the church. The soldiers jerked a picture of Christ from the wall and ordered each person to come to the front and spit on the picture. The first man to walk down the aisle was a deacon. He looked at the picture for a few seconds, quickly spat, and walked to one side. Three others did the same. The fifth person to walk forward was a young teenaged girl. She looked at the picture of Christ and then bent down and wiped the spit off with her skirt. She hugged the picture of Jesus to her heart and said 'Shoot me, I am ready to die.' The soldiers couldn't shoot. They ordered everyone to get out. The people overheard the communist soldiers say to the girl, 'You are not fit to live. If you had a chance to renounce communism, you would do the same thing.' Shortly afterwards the people heard four shots. Because of the strong faith of one girl, the rest of the village was saved.

Themes: Martyrs, Persecution, Sacrifice, Suffering.

Scriptures: Daniel 3:16–18; Matthew 25:14–30; Mark 8:34–38; 11:22–24; Luke 7:1–10; Acts 4:1–22; 6:8–8:3; 7:54–8:8; 9:23–25; 14:5–6, 19; 16:19–24; 21:30–36; 1 Corinthians 4:11–13; 13:3; 2 Corinthians 6:4–5; 11:23–28; 1 Thessalonians 2:9; 2 Thessalonians 3:8.

40: *Faithfulness*

A minister and two girls were sentenced to death by the Chinese communists. The minister was promised release if he would shoot the girls. He accepted. On the day of the execution in the courtyard the girls whispered to each other, then bowed respectfully before the minister. One of them said 'Before being shot by you, we wish to thank you heartily for what you have meant to us. You baptised us, you taught us the way of eternal life, you gave us Holy Communion with the same hand in which you now have the gun. May God reward you for all the good you have done us. You also taught us that Christians are sometimes weak and commit terrible sins, but they can be forgiven again. When you regret what you are about to do to us, do not despair like Judas, but repent like Peter. God bless you, and remember that our last thought was not one of indignation against your failure. Everyone passes through hours of darkness. We die with gratitude.'

The minister then shot the girls. Afterwards he was shot by the communists.

Themes: Betrayal, Forgiveness, Judas, Martyrdom, Persecution, Revenge, Suffering.

Scriptures: Matthew 5:43–48; 25:14–30; 27:3–10; Mark 8:34–38; 11:22–25; 14:10–11, 43–50; Luke 7:1–10; Acts 7:54–8:8; Romans 12:12, 14.

41: Failure

There is a sixty-year-old student in Germany who is finding study a bit too demanding. He has been given one last chance to pass his exams. He has been studying the same course for more than forty years. And since 1949 he has failed more than 250 exam papers.

A spokesman at Göttingen University said it was 'about time he took up some other career and made room for a youngster'.

Themes: Encouragement, Examinations, Humour, Sin – missing the mark, Students, Study, Success, Perseverance, University.

Scriptures: Psalm 51; John 8:34–36, 46; Romans 5:12; 6:12, 14; 7:17; 8:2; 12:11; James 1:15; 1 John 1:18.

42: *Family*

Diane's father was a well-respected lawyer in the community. But he was a terror to live with. Verbally and sometimes physically abusive, he was always critical and unreachable.

When she was nine, her mother caught her father in the midst of an affair. In a fit of anger, she threatened to expose her husband and ruin his reputation in their small town. But, like a wounded lion, he turned on her and successfully sued *her* for divorce first. He thoroughly slandered her name in the process.

Their 'soap-opera' courtroom theatrics became so bad that other parents forbade their children to play or even talk with Diane or her older brother at school. Then, one day, circumstances turned from bad to far worse. When Diane and her brother came home from school, the removal men were in the house packing all their things and getting ready to cart them away. Their father had won the divorce decree and had even obtained a court order evicting his former wife from the house

As the mother wept, Diane's older brother became furious. He stormed into the house, up to his father's room, and grabbed a gun he knew his father always hid in his bedside drawer. When he came out of the house, his grandmother was walking up the porch and saw him with the gun. In a burst of anger he told her he was on the way to kill his father. She grabbed at him, trying to wrestle the gun away. But in the struggle the gun went off. In a terrible accident Diane's brother had killed his own grandmother.

Tragedy would follow tragedy that day. When the police came to the house, they tracked down the boy who was hiding in a neighbour's garage. A gun battle broke out. An officer was critically wounded and Diane's brother was killed.

Only nine years old, Diane had lived through the trauma of her parents' hostile divorce. She had lost her grandmother and her brother in a single day. There was nothing good about what happened to Diane or her family. The pain caused by her father and brother will always be with her. What a terrible marriage partner she would make with such a background.

'Yet,' she says, 'it has taken many years, but I can actually say that God has used my childhood to make me a better person, especially with my own family. I have had to work through a lot, but I know God has made me a more loving wife and mother because of what I have been through.'

Themes: Adultery, Anger, Divorce, Families, Healing – inner, Marriage, Murder, Trauma, Violence – domestic.

Scriptures: Deuteronomy 6:20–25; Psalms 91; 118:5–6; Matthew 5:21–26; Mark 10:2–12; Luke 8:22–25; Romans 12:10, 16, 17–18; Ephesians 6:1–4; Colossians 3:18–21.

43: Fathers

Phillip Adams is an Australian journalist and radio announcer. There was a day in his school life that sums up what he knows about fathers.

To the outside world his dad was all charm and decency; to

him and his mum he was nothing but a sadist. His parents' marriage flew apart and he ended up with a step-dad.

Phillip says that the most horrific day of his childhood was when he set out to see his dad and meet his new wife. She was supposed to look like a film star. But, just before Phillip left home for the railway station, there was a huge fight between his mum and his step-father. He knocked his step-father over to save his mum. In fact he sent him flying across the room, pounding into the venetian blinds and leaving them buckled for ever.

Phillip ran from the house in fear. His step-dad charged after him in his big black car and tried to run him down. He only saved himself by hurling himself into the grass by the side of the road and hiding until he went away. However, to his horror, at the next train station on the way to his dad's, there was that lunatic face in the window and his hand on the door. It was peak period and it seemed as if there were thousands of people milling around watching. He dragged Phillip out of the carriage, threw out the suitcase, scattered everything, screamed to everyone that Phillip was a thief. Then he switched with his usual skill, to being sweetly reasonable. He apologised to the crowd which was becoming a bit menacing. He became tearful and said that he would take Phillip to his father in his car. The train had long gone. Phillip begged people not to let him put him in the car. But into the car he went. As they were going past the police station Phillip flung himself out of the car.

Somehow Phillip got himself to his father's that night. His 'film star' step-mother turned out to be more like the witch from *The Wizard of Oz*.

He will never forget walking down the path to the little house his father had. Through the window he could see this extraordinary woman trying to stab his dad with a pair of scissors. His father was screaming like a stuffed pig in terror. As he ran out of the door in horror Phillip ran in and knocked her unconscious. That was his first meeting with his step-mother. He and his father went and sat in the car.

He remembers shaking and crying with the accumulated horror of the day. That day summed up Phillip's experience of a father.

Themes: Adultery, Anger, Divorce, Families, Family relationships, Rejection, Marriage, Mothers, Murder, Parenting, Trauma, Violence – domestic.

Scriptures: 6:20–25; Matthew 5:21–32; Mark 10:2–12; Romans 12:10, 16, 17–18; Ephesians 6:1–4; Colossians 3:18–21.

44: *Forgiven*

It had been the custom of a kindly doctor to go through his book from time to time noting those who had not paid. When he realised that the debts remained because the patients could not pay he put a red line through the debt and wrote by the side of it, 'Forgiven, unable to pay'.

After his death, his wife was looking through his books and saw all the marks and said to herself, 'My husband was owed a lot of money. I could do with that money now.' She took the matter to the local court to sue the debtors of the money. The judge, however, looked at the doctor's account book and said, 'No court in the world will give you a verdict against those people when your husband, with his own pen has written, "Forgiven, unable to pay."'

Themes: Debt, Doctors, Grace, Mercy, Parables – unforgiving servant, Pardon, Release.

Scriptures: Exodus 34:9; Numbers 14:19–20; Psalm 25:11, 51; Nehemiah 9:17; Isaiah 55:7; 40:2; Matthew 18:21–35; Mark 2:1–12; 1 John 1:9.

45: Forgiveness

It was when leaving Greenwich in her barge to set out on her progress on 17 July, 1579 that Queen Elizabeth I nearly lost her life. She was heading, Stow records in his *Annals*, with Lord Lincoln and the French ambassador, for Deptford. 'It chanced that one Thomas Appletree, with two or three children of Her Majesty's Chapel, was rowing up and down this reach with a caliver [gun], shooting at random, very rashly.' He must have been unbelievably careless in his aim, for one of his random shots passed within six feet of the Queen, piercing one of her watermen clean through both his arms and knocking him out of his seat. This not unnaturally 'forced him to cry out and screech out piteously, supposing himself to be slain'. Elizabeth showed herself equal to the occasion, and, seeing him maimed, 'she never bashed thereat, but bid him be of good cheer, and said he would want of nothing that might be for his ease'. Young Appletree, however, was given a terrible lesson. He was condemned to death, and four days later, brought to the gallows which had been set up by the waterside near the scene of his crime. But 'when the hangman had put the rope about his neck, he was, by the Queen's most gracious pardon, delivered from execution'.

Themes: Capital punishment, Debt, Grace, Mercy, Pardon, Release, Sin.

Scriptures: Exodus 34:9, Numbers 14:19–20; 1 Kings 8:22–53; 2 Chronicles 6:12–42; Nehemiah 9:17; Psalms 25:11; 51; 103:3; Jeremiah 31:34; 36:3; Daniel 9:19; Amos 7:2; Isaiah 55:7; 40:2; Matthew 6:12, 14, 15; 18:21–35; Mark 2:1–12; 11:25; John 8:34–36; Romans 5; Ephesians 2:8; 1 John 1:9.

46: *Forgiveness*

In ancient times, if a person became bankrupt, the list of his debts was written on a parchment and nailed up in a public place. There was a nail at the top and another at the bottom of the parchment. A rich friend seeing this humiliating document could take out the bottom nail, double up the parchment in two, write his name across the folded document and drive the bottom nail in to secure the folded parchment. The signature across the document meant that the person would take responsibility for his friend's debt.

Themes: Freedom, Grace, Mercy, Pardon, Release, Sin.

Scriptures: Exodus 34:9; Numbers 14:19–20; 1 Kings 8:22–33; 2 Chronicles 6:12–42; Nehemiah 9:17; Psalms 25:11; 51; 103:3; Jeremiah 31:34; 36:3; Daniel 9:19; Amos 7:2; Isaiah 55:7; 40:2; Matthew 6:12, 14, 15; 18:21–35; 26:28; Mark 1:4; 2:1–12; 11:25; Luke 1:77; 3:3; 4:18; 24:47; John 8:31–36; Acts 2:38; 5:31; 10:43; 13:38; 26:18; Romans 5; Ephesians 2:8; Colossians 1:14; 1 John 1:9.

47: *Forgiveness*

Some years ago, God began dealing with the attitude that Paul Cho, the Korean, had towards Japan, the long-standing enemy of Korea.

Paul Cho was invited to speak to a group of ministers in Japan. When he got up to speak, he tried to say nice things about Japan but could not. He began to weep. A deep silence filled the audience of ministers. He looked up and confessed how he felt.

'I must confess that I hate you all. I don't hate you personally, but I hate the fact that you are Japanese. I know that this is wrong, but this is the way I honestly feel. Won't you please forgive me? I am repenting of my sin and ask you to pray for me.'

With these words spoken, he simply bowed his head and began to cry aloud. When he looked up he saw that all the ministers were crying too. After a few minutes, one of the Japanese ministers stood and said, 'Dr Cho, we as Japanese take full responsibility for the sins of our fathers. Will you please forgive us?'

Paul Cho came down from the platform and threw his arms around the man who had just spoken.

'Yes I forgive you and I commit myself to pray for you and Japan.'

Cho says that he instantly felt healed of the bitterness that he had felt since he was a child. He was free.

Themes: Bitterness, Confession, Enemies, Freedom, Hate, Inner healing, Lord's Prayer, Love.

Scriptures: 1 Samuel 12:1–15; Psalm 51; Proverbs 28:13; Matthew 5:43–48; 6:5–15; 18:21–35; Mark 2:1–12; 11:25; Luke 10:27; John 8:31–36; Romans 12:14; 1 Corinthians 13; Galatians 5:1; James 5:16.

48: Forgiveness

I started to read Fine Arts, which I enjoyed, but I found myself drifting more and more into the amateur theatrical life of the campus. The Union Theatre was small but well equipped and I spent most of my time there. We were rehearsing, I think, a production of Hecht's *The Front Page* when a strange cathartic event occurred. Standing at the stage door and looking across an expanse of lawn towards the medical school, I saw a vaguely familiar figure sitting studiously beneath a gum tree reading. I experienced a painful flashback to Grade One at Camberwell Grammar. It was John Bromley, the boy with the soft slug-like skin who delighted in giving me 'chinese burns' and 'rabbit choppers', the archetypal bully of my childhood.

How quiet and peaceful he seemed now, poring over his book in the feathery shadow of the foliage. I descended immediately to the room beneath the stage used for storing scene-painting equipment. Looking quickly around, I saw a large sack of white powder and, seizing this, I lugged it upstairs and out of the stage door. Bromley still sat there in deep shadow. He hadn't moved. Very quickly, with my heart pounding, I crept stealthily towards him until I was directly behind him, and then raised and tilted the heavy sack. A twig cracked sharply under my foot and Bromley looked around and up. By then the bag was evacuating a dense cascade of pigment over the seated student. Just when I thought the whole torrent was petering out, it seemed to renew itself. When the bag was finally empty, I turned and cravenly bolted, only once glancing over my shoulder. Standing now, though seemingly rooted to the spot, stood a totally white figure under a tree.

Back in my dressing-room, slightly puffed, I experienced the voluptuous satisfaction of vengeance. I remembered, with intense pleasure also, the victim's face as it turned towards me in that instant before the clown-white avalanche struck. It was *not* Bromley. Not, in fact, much like Bromley at all. But thereafter Bromley was forgiven. That blanched and bewildered figure on the Union lawn had unwittingly performed a noble act of expiation.

Themes: Cross, Easter, Expiation, Revenge, Substitution.

Scriptures: Isaiah 53; Matthew 5:43–48; Mark 10:45; 11:25; Romans 3:21–25; John 11:50; Galatians 3:13; 1 Timothy 2:6; Hebrews 9:28; 1 Peter 2:24.

49: *Forgiveness*

Corrie Ten Boom's family hid Jews above their family watchmaker's shop until she and her sister Betsie were arrested by the Nazis and put in Ravensbrück concentration camp. There Betsie died.

After the war Corrie was speaking in a church in Münich. Then, as she shook hands with people, she found herself confronted by a man she recognised as having been a guard in the camp. She heard him saying, 'You mentioned Ravensbrück in your talk. I was a guard there. But since that time I have become a Christian. I know that God has forgiven me for the cruel things I did there, but I would like to hear it from your lips as well. Fräulein, will you forgive me?'

Corrie says that she could not. Betsie had died in that place. Could he erase her slow terrible death simply for the asking? Corrie says that it could not have been many seconds that he stood there, hand held out. But to her it seemed hours as she wrestled with the most difficult decision she had ever had to make.

She stood there with the coldness clutching her heart. But she knew that forgiveness is not an emotion, it is an act of the will – she had to hand on the forgiveness she knew.

'Jesus help me,' she prayed silently. 'I can lift my hand; I can do that much. You supply the feeling.'

So woodenly, mechanically, she thrust her hand into the one outstretched to her and offered the forgiveness God had given her. As she did, an incredible thing took place. She says that the current started in her shoulder, raced down her arm and sprang into their joined hands. Then a healing warmth seemed to flood her whole being, bringing tears to her eyes.

'I forgive you, brother,' she cried, 'with all my heart!'

For a long moment they grasped each other's hands, the former guard and the former prisoner. Corrie had never known God's love so intensely as she did then. She was able to forgive as she had been forgiven.

Themes: Forgiveness handed on, God's love, Lord's Prayer, Reconciliation.

Scriptures: Psalm 51; Matthew 6:5–15; 18:21–35; Mark 11:25; Romans 12:14; 1 Thessalonians 5:13.

50: Forgiveness – necessary

Some years ago, John Wimber was asked to pray for healing for a woman in her late forties. She suffered from chronic stomach disorders and arthritis. When John started to pray over her he received insight that she was bitter. So he asked her if she was feeling hostility, anger or bitterness towards someone; and he felt led to ask specifically if she had felt that way towards her sister.

She stiffened up, then said, 'No. I haven't seen my sister for sixteen years.'

John enquired further, 'Are you sure?'

Then she told John how years ago her sister had married a man she loved, then later divorced him. 'I cannot forgive my sister for that,' she admitted.

'If you don't forgive her,' John told her, 'your bones will waste away, just as David complained his did when he kept silent about his sin of adultery with Bathsheba.'

When she heard his words she relented. 'What should I do?' she asked.

John Wimber told her to write her sister a letter, forgiving her and asking to renew their relationship. She wrote the letter immediately, but she did not post it for several weeks. During that time she became more ill, until she thought she was going to die. Then she remembered the letter. Somehow she summoned the strength to drive to the post office and post it. The very *moment* she dropped the letter in the box, she experienced relief, and she was completely healed by the time she reached home.

Theme: Anger, Bitterness, Healing, Hostility, Reconciliation,

Relationships, Resentment, Sickness.

Scriptures: 2 Samuel 11; Psalm 32; 51; Matthew 5:22–24; 6:5–51; 18:21–35; Mark 2:1–12; 11:25; Romans 12:14; 1 Corinthians 11:29–32; 13; 1 Thessalonians 5:13.

51: *Forgiveness – refused*

During the presidency of Andrew Jackson, George Wilson, a postal clerk, robbed a federal payroll from a train and in the process killed a guard. The court convicted Wilson and sentenced him to hang. Because of public sentiment against capital punishment, however, a movement began to secure a presidential pardon for Wilson (first offence), and eventually President Jackson intervened with a pardon. Amazingly, Wilson refused it.

Since this had never happened before, the Supreme Court was asked to rule on whether a person could refuse a presidential pardon. Chief Justice John Marshall handed down the court's decision: 'A pardon is a parchment whose only value must be determined by the receiver of the pardon. It has no value apart from that which the receiver gives to it. George Wilson has refused to accept the pardon. We cannot conceive why he would do so, but he has. Therefore, George Wilson must die.'

George Wilson, as punishment for his crime, was hanged.

Pardon, declared the Supreme Court, must not only be granted, it must be accepted.

Theme: Capital punishment, Grace, Pardon, Sin.

Scriptures: 1 Kings 8:22–53; 2 Chronicles 6:12–42; Psalm 103:3; Jeremiah 31:34; 36:3; Daniel 9:19; Amos 7:2; Mark 10:17–22; 11:25; John 8:34–36; Romans 5; Ephesians 2:8.

52: *Forgiveness – transforms*

The musical *Les Misérables* follows Victor Hugo's sprawling novel. It recounts the story of Jean Valjean, a French prisoner hounded and eventually transformed.

Jean served a nineteen-year jail term of hard labour for stealing a loaf of bread to feed his hungry family. He entered the French penal system as an impressionable young man. He emerged tough, hardened and embittered by the experience. No one could beat Jean in a fistfight. No one could break his will.

After serving this term, he was at last, set free. But convicts in those days had to carry identity cards. No innkeeper would let a dangerous felon like Jean spend the night in his establishment. For four days he wandered the village roads seeking shelter. Finally, a kindly bishop had mercy on him.

That night Jean lay still in a comfortable bed until the bishop and his sister had drifted off to sleep. Then he rose, rummaged through the cupboards for the family silver, and crept off in the darkness with six silver plates and a silver soup ladle – the bishop's pride and joy.

The next morning, three policemen knocked on the bishop's door. Jean was with them. They had found the convict running away, with the stolen silver in his bag. Jean's unlikely story was that the bishop had given him the silver. The police were ready to put the scoundrel in chains for life. Jean had failed to live up to the new life he was offered.

However, the bishop did the very opposite to what the gendarme, or Jean, expected. The bishop greeted Jean like a worthy friend.

'So here you are! I am delighted to see you. Have you forgotten that I gave you the candlesticks as well? They're silver like the rest, and worth a good 200 francs. Did you forget to take them?' Jean's eyes widened in disbelief. He was now staring at the old bishop with an expression for which there were no words.

The bishop turned to assure the police. 'This silver was my gift to him.' Satisfied, the gendarmes withdrew.

The bishop did not change when he was alone with Jean. Indeed, he gave the candlesticks to his guest who was now speechless and trembling. He said to Jean, 'Do not forget, do not ever forget, that you have promised me to use the money to make yourself an honest man.'

The next day, Jean's knee buckled under him as if an invisible power overwhelmed him as a blow, with the weight of his bad conscience. He fell exhausted on a large stone, his hands clenched in his hair, and his face on his knees. 'What a wretch I am!' he cried.

Then his heart swelled and he burst into tears. It was the first time he had cried in nineteen years. He wept long and bitterly; with more weakness than a woman and with more tenderness than a child. At first there were tears of remorse and guilt. Then, as he cried, the light grew brighter and brighter in his mind – an extraordinary light, a light transporting and terrible.

A revengeful detective stalked Jean for the next twenty years in an attempt to catch him out. But, repentance and forgiveness had transformed Jean. He became the dignified and respected mayor of the town. The detective could find nothing and eventually threw himself off a bridge into the Seine.

Theme: Confession, Debt, Grace, Mercy, Pardon, Release, Remorse, Repentance, Revenge, Theft, Transformed.

Scriptures: Exodus 34:9; Numbers 14:19–20; 1 Kings 8:22–53; 2 Chronicles 6:12–42; Nehemiah 9:17; Psalms 25:11; 51; 103:3; Isaiah 40:2; 55:7; Jeremiah 31:34; 36:3; Daniel 9:19; Amos 7:2; Matthew 5:43–48; 6:12, 14, 15; 18:21–35; Mark 2:1–12; 11:25; Romans 5; Ephesians 2:8; 1 John 1:9.

53: Freed

In the time of the Napoleonic wars, a man who did not want to go was balloted as a conscript. But he had a friend who wanted to go to war and so went in his place. The friend was killed in battle and buried on the battlefield. Some time later there was another ballot to obtain conscripts. By some mistake the first man was balloted a second time. He refused to go.

'You cannot take me,' he said.

'Why not?' they asked.

'I am dead,' was his reply.

'You are not dead you are alive and well.'

'But I am dead,' he insisted.

'Why, man, you are mad. Where did you die?'

'At the battlefield. And you left me buried on the field.'

'You talk like a mad man,' they cried.

But the man stuck to his point; that he had been dead and buried several months.

'You look up your records,' he said, 'and see if it is not so.'

They looked and found that he was right. They found the man's name entered as drafted and sent to war and marked off as killed.

'Look here,' they said, 'you did not die. You must have got someone to go for you. It must have been your substitute.'

'I know that,' he said. 'He died in my place. You cannot touch me. I can go free. The law has no claim against me.'

The authorities would not accept this, and the case was actually taken to Napoleon. He ruled that the man was right. Legally, even though through a substitute, he had died and was buried on the battlefield. France had no claim on him.

Theme: Atonement, Christ – our representative, Christ – our substitute, Christ – our ransom, Forgiveness.

Scriptures: Isaiah 53; Mark 10:45; 11:25; Luke 1:68; 2:38; Romans 3:21–25; John 11:50; Galatians 3:13; 1 Timothy 2:6; Hebrews 9:11–14, 28; 1 Peter 2:24.

54: Generosity

George Carey was once involved in a church rebuilding programme in Durham in the north of England.

'One day,' he says, 'I went to the front door to find a big bulky envelope on the mat. In it was £400 from an old-age pensioner who had been left some money. There was also a note. "A thanksgiving for the church which has meant so much to me. This is given that others may share the faith that has helped me."'

Theme: Giving, Materialism, Money, Sacrificial giving, Tithing, Wealth.

Scriptures: Malachi 3:6–12; Mark 10:17–31; 2:41–44; Luke 19:1–10; 2 Corinthians 8 and 9; 1 Timothy 6:17–19; Hebrews 13:5.

55: Generosity

A woman was invited to a Zulu church. She went, and was conspicuous as the only white person there. They welcomed her, translated for her, and made her thoroughly at home. They had a collection to build a new Zulu church down the road. Later in the service, they had another collection for Zulu Christian brethren who had no shoes. By this time, she had put in all the money she had with her. Imagine how staggered she was when they had a third collection. She had nothing left. But the collection was announced 'for petrol for our white sister'. That woman came out with an entirely new perspective on Christian giving.

Theme: Giving, God – his provision, Offerings, Materialism, Money, Sacrificial giving, Tithing, Wealth.

Scriptures: Psalm 112:9; Isaiah 55:10–11; Mark 10:17–31; 12:41–44; Luke 19:1–10; 2 Corinthians 8 and 9; 1 Timothy 6:17–19; Hebrews 13:5.

56: Gifts of the Spirit – using

On 27 May, 1840, Niccolo Paganini, perhaps the greatest violinist of all time, lay dying. He reached slowly from his bed to hold just once more the instrument he loved best. But as his fingers lightly brushed over the vibrant strings, Paganini died. He was fifty-eight.

A few days later, on 1 June, his will was opened and read. It disposed of a fortune of roughly two million lire (about £80,000), a valuable collection of jewellery, instruments, and a large amount of property and securities across several European countries. After providing generously for his sisters, everything else was to go to his son, Baron Achille Paganini. However, the will directed that Paganini's favourite Guarneri violin be preserved in the Municipal Museum of Genoa.

His son fought hard to retain his favourite instrument, the last thing touched by the great master. But the city fathers of Genoa refused to waive the right given them by the will. Achille offered the city the fine marble bust Varni had made, in place of the violin; the mayor refused.

To this day the violin is very rarely played, standing in a glass case surrounded by other relics of the great man.

Theme: Body, Hidden talents.

Scriptures: Matthew 25:14–30; Romans 12:3–6; 1 Corinthians 12:12–27; Ephesians 4:12–16; 1 Peter 4:7–11.

57: *Gifts of the Spirit – using*

Antonio Stradivari has not been surpassed in the making of violins, even though he died in 1737.

In 1716 he built an instrument which became his favourite, and it never left him. When he died it passed into the hands of his sons Francesco and Paola. Then it was sold to Count Cozio di Salabue in 1775, and valued at about £100.

In 1827 Luigi Tarisio, the famous collector, purchased it. But then it was not seen for decades.

It received the name 'La Messie' (the Messiah) for those hearing the raptures of Tarisio became sceptical of there being such an instrument, as no one had ever set eyes upon it.

One morning in 1854, Luigi Tarisio was found dead. 246 exquisite violins were found in the place. Some were crammed in the attic. One – the best one – was found in the bottom drawer of an old rickety bureau.

When the greatest Stradivarius, 'La Messie' was brought out and played, it had been cruelly silent for 147 years. But the silence still continues. In 1931 the instrument was purchased by W.E. Hill and Sons for £2,000. In 1938 it was presented by them to the Ashmolean Museum in Oxford to be kept in perpetuity in a room especially prepared for it. Luigi Tarisio and other collectors have robbed the world of the sound of this violin.

Theme: Body, Evangelism – failure, Hidden talents.

Scriptures: Matthew 25:14–30; Romans 12:3–6; 1 Corinthians 12:12–27; Ephesians 4:12–16; 1 Peter 4:7–11.

58: Giving

The late R.G. LeTourneau, the great Texas industrialist, had the gift of giving. The key question in relation to the gift of giving is described in his autobiography. In it he said 'The question is not how much of my money I give to God, but rather how much of God's money I keep.' He answered it in his life by turning 90% of the assets of the company over to his Christian foundation, and then he and his wife gave in cash 90% of the income that was realised from the share of the business that he kept. He and his wife never lacked.

Theme: Giving, God – his provision, Materialism, Money, Offerings, Sacrificial giving, Tithing, Wealth.

Scriptures: Psalm 112:9; Isaiah 55:10–11; Mark 10:17–31; 12:41–44; Luke 19:1–10; 2 Corinthians 8 and 9; 1 Timothy 6:17–19; Hebrews 13:5.

59: Giving

Graham and Treena Kerr were wealthy and famous when they first came to know the Lord. You probably remember Graham from his TV show 'The Galloping Gourmet'. When they were converted, God told them to give away everything, and they did – millions of dollars. They were rich young rulers who obeyed.

What was surprising was the criticism they recieved from Christians because of their obedience. Some charged them with not being good stewards. They said they should have invested it so they could continue to give more and more.

Such responses show where people's real values lie, like the disciples when the woman broke the expensive alabaster vial of perfume over Jesus' head, they said 'This money could have been better spent!'

Theme: Giving, God – his provision, Offerings, Money.

Scriptures: Psalm 112:9; Isaiah 55:10; Mark 10:17–31; 11:22–24; 12:41–44; Luke 7:1–10; 19:1–10; 2 Corinthians 8 and 9; 1 Timothy 6:17–19; Hebrews 13:5.

60: *God – access to him*

During the American Civil War, as a result of family tragedy, a soldier had been granted permission to seek a hearing from the president. He wanted to request exemption from military service. However, when he arrived at the White House he was refused entry and sent away. He went and sat in a nearby park.

A young boy came across him and remarked how unhappy he looked. The soldier found himself telling the young lad everything. Eventually the boy said 'Come with me.' He led the dejected soldier back to the White House. They went around the back, none of the guards stopping them. Even the generals and high-ranking government officials stood to attention and let them pass through. The soldier was amazed.

Finally, they came to the presidential office. Without knocking, the young boy opened the door and walked straight in. Abraham Lincoln, standing there, turned from his conversation with the Secretary of State and said, 'What can I do for you, Todd?'

Todd said, 'Dad, this soldier needs to talk to you.'

Theme: Access, Holy of Holies – entrance to, Jesus – the high priest, Prayer.

Scriptures: Romans 5:2; Ephesians 2:18; Hebrews 4:14–5:10.

61: *God – his existence*

Isaac Newton was a Professor of Maths in Cambridge from 1669 to 1701. He is said to be one of the greatest scientists of all time. He did much of his brilliant original work in his parents' home in Lincolnshire immediately after he graduated from university. The University was closed for a couple of years during the great plague.

His most far-reaching achievement was the formulation of the universal law of gravitation, explainig the motion and behaviour of planets. Newton was also a fine Christian.

It is said that one day he was sitting at his desk working. One of his atheist friends came in to see Newton in his room. To one side there was a beautifully made orrery – a clockwork model to demonstrate the movement of the planets around the sun. During the conversation the atheist was admiring this complicated and beautifully crafted machine. Eventually he asked Newton, 'Who made the orrery?'

'Oh, no one,' said Newton. 'It just happened!'

Theme: Atheists, God – creator.

Scriptures: Psalm 53:1; Isaiah 40:12–26; Jeremiah 10:11–16; Acts 17:24–29; Romans 1:19–20.

62: *God – his existence*

A young communist was showing a Christian around Moscow. After a time the communist chided the Christian for his belief in God. 'I'm astonished,' he said, 'that an intelligent person like you can possibly believe in a foolish myth like that!'

The Christian said nothing, paused for a moment, and then grabbed the communist by the wrist. 'Look at your watch!' he said. 'See its precision and accuracy. Think of the incredibly delicate nature of its mechanism. But according to your reasoning it just happened. It all fell into place by chance. There was no maker or designer behind it!'

The communist appeared startled. He said nothing.

'Now look at your hand,' continued the Christian. 'Look at the fantastic mechanism of your hand. It is a thousand times, a million times more wonderful than your watch. Yet, according to your reasoning, it just happened! It all fell into place by chance. There was no maker or designer behind it. Now I am astonished that an intelligent person like you can believe that your watch was created, but that your hand was not. And that's just your hand, let alone the rest of your body, or the rest of creation!'

Themes: Atheists, Communism, God – creator, God – existence of.

Scriptures: Psalm 53:1; Isaiah 40:12–26; Jeremiah 10:11–16; Acts 17:24–29; Romans 1:19–20.

63: *God – his existence*

In her will, an eccentric woman who lived in Cherokee County, North Carolina, gave her entire estate to God. The court was forced to issue a summons, and the sheriff went through the motions of trying to serve it. His report, filed in the Cherokee County Court, reads: 'After due and diligent search, God cannot be found in Cherokee County.'

Themes: Atheists, Death, God – creator, God – search for, Wills.

Scriptures: Psalm 53:1; Isaiah 40:12–26; Jeremiah 10:11–16; John 11:25–26; Acts 17:24–29; Romans 1:19–20.

64: *God – his existence*

The story is told of a man who walked too near the edge of a cliff. He fell off, and as he plunged down, he put out his hand and hung onto a thorn bush growing from the cliff face. He looked up – the cliff was too high to climb. He looked down – it was too far to fall!

In desperation he looked up again and shouted, 'Is anyone there?' To his delight, there was an answering voice. 'Yes, I – the Lord your God – am here.'

'What shall I do?' called the man.

After a pause, the voice replied, 'Let go.'

The man looked down at the rocks 100 metres below. Then he looked up, and called out again, 'Is there anyone else up there?'

Themes: Atheists, Faith, God – his care, Trust.

Scriptures: Psalms 37:3–5; 53:1; 145: 14–21; Proverbs 3:5–6; Isaiah 40:12–26; Jeremiah 10:11–16; Matthew 6:25–34; Mark 11:22–24; Luke 7:1–10; Acts 17:24–29; Romans 1:19–20.

65: *God – his existence*

William Paley was a lecturer in Oxford and then a priest in Carlisle in the eighteenth century. He is virtually forgotten now except for his famous example of argument from design for

God's existence. He begins his book *Natural Theology* with a parable.

Suppose a man is walking across a moor and he happens to hit his foot against a watch. He picks it up; he has never seen a watch before; he examines it. He sees that the hands are moving round the dial in what is clearly an orderly way. He opens it up and he finds inside a host of wheels and cogs and levers and springs and jewels. He discovers that by winding up the watch, you can set it going, and that the whole complicated machinery is moving in what is obviously a predetermined pattern. What then does he say, 'By chance all these wheels and levers and jewels and springs came together and formed themselves into this thing I have in my hand. By chance they set themselves going. By chance they move in an orderly way. By chance this watch became an instrument which counts the hours and minutes and seconds'? No. If he applies his mind to this problem at all, he says, 'I have found a watch. *Somewhere there must be a watch-maker.*' So then, when we discover a world where there is an order more accurate than my watch, where tides ebb and flow according to schedule, where spring, summer, autumn and winter come back in unvarying succession, where the planets never leave their courses, where the same cause always produces the same effects, we are bound to say, 'I have found a world. *Somewhere there must be a world-maker.*'

Themes: Atheists, God – creator.

Scriptures: Psalm 53:1; Isaiah 40:12–26; Jeremiah 10:11–16; Acts 17:24–29; Romans 1:19–20.

66: God – knowledge of us

A little boy and his dad were doing some shopping. The little fellow was keen to carry the wire basket. The father loaded up the basket with one thing after another. A shopper stopped and whispered some light-hearted sympathy in the little fellow's ear about the basket being a bit heavy for him. But the boy looked up and had this to say, 'It's OK, my dad knows how much I can carry.'

Themes: God – care of us, God – as father.

Scriptures: Psalms 103; 121; 139; 145:9; Jeremiah 23:24; Jonah 1:3; Acts 14:17.

67: God's love – free

A mother gave her son a ticket to the football match. However, instead of enjoying the game, he spent the entire time walking around the ground collecting cans and bottles to pay her back for the price of the ticket.

'We didn't want him to work during the game,' the mother said sadly. 'We wanted him to enjoy it.'

She said, 'I'll never forget his sweaty little face as he told me he lacked only two bottles before he could pay us back. His father and I had thought that all the time he was enjoying the ballgame with his friends.'

Themes: Earning God's favour, Forgiveness, God – his love, Grace, Works, God – his favour.

Scriptures: Psalm 143:2; Mark 11:25; Luke 10:27; Acts 10:43; Romans 1:17; 3:20; 1 Corinthians 13; Galatians 2:16; Ephesians 2:1–10.

68: *God – with us*

During the First World War a soldier in the trenches saw his friend out in no man's land stumble and fall in a hail of bullets. He said to his officer, 'May I go, sir, and bring him in?' But the officer refused. 'No one can live out there,' he said. 'I should only lose you as well.' Disobeying the order, the man went to try to save his friend, for they had been like David and Jonathan throughout the whole war. Somehow he got his friend onto his shoulder and staggered back to the trenches, but he himself lay mortally wounded and his friend was dead.

The officer was angry. 'I told you not to go,' he said. 'Now I have lost both of you. It was not worth it.'

With his dying breath the man said, 'But it was worth it.'

'Worth it!' said the officer. 'How could it be? Your friend is dead and you are mortally wounded.'

The boy shrank from reproach, but looking up into the officer's face, he said, 'It was worth it, sir, because when I got to him, he said "Jim, I knew you'd come."'

Themes: Atonement, Compassion, Friendship, Redemption, Rescue, Ransom, War.

Scriptures: Exodus 15:2; Psalms 27:1; 34:4; 46; 62:2; Isaiah 42:13–53:12; 60:19; Matthew 6:19–34; 10:28; Mark 10:45; John 11:50; Romans 3:21–25; Galatians 3:13; Philippians 4:6; 1 Timothy 2:6; 2 Timothy 1:7; Hebrews 9:28; 13:5–6; 1 Peter 2:21–25; 5:5–6.

69: Good news – eager to hear

Early in January 1940, two men found their way to Mission Hospital in India. They said they had come on behalf of their village to ask for someone to be sent to tell them about Christianity. Lesslie Newbigin continues the story:

> Two or three days later three of us set off ... for the village ... In the middle of the village was a small, well-built temple. To our surprise, the temple was immediately opened, a lamp brought, and ourselves invited to sit down inside. In a few minutes a large crowd was gathered round the porch of the temple, and the leading man ... spoke to us.... 'We have invited you to come, and we are glad that you have come. Now here we are, and we know nothing about Christianity, but we want you to tell us all about it from the beginning.'

One of those with Newbigin began from the idol in whose temple they were sitting and went on to announce the good news of Jesus. A church had begun.

Themes: Evangelism, Idols, India, Missionaries, Witnessing.

Scriptures: Matthew 28:16–20; Mark 3:13–19; 6:7–13; Luke 9:1–6; 10:1–20; Acts 10:1–48; 17:16–23.

70 : Grace – sufficient

Three-year-old Mandy was born into the home of Marshall and Susan Shelley. Mandy was severely and profoundly retarded due to microcephaly.

Marshall and Susan desperately prayed that Mandy would develop some skills. But, eventually, they had to accept that

Mandy would never talk, nor walk, nor sit up, nor use her hands. She suffered frequent seizures. She stopped swallowing so they learned to administer medication and formula through a tube surgically implanted in her stomach. The parents never knew if she could see or hear. On the outside Mandy may not have appeared valuable. Yet, as they and other folk loved and cared for Mandy, something happened to them.

When the Shelleys arrived at church several sets of arms would reach out to take her. People you wouldn't expect – teenage boys, a woman recently widowed, men who didn't usually exhibit much interest in babies – would take turns in cuddling her. After church they would have to hunt for her as she had been passed from lap to lap.

The Shelleys and those near them had many questions. Why was such a child born? What is her future? There were no easy answers. But in loving and caring for Mandy, people were set free.

For example, after observing Mandy, one hospital employee said she decided 'to get God in my life', as she put it.

In February 1992, Mandy contracted viral pneumonia. Her body did not have the strength to shake it. One Thursday, Susan and Marshall sat in Mandy's room, taking turns holding her. A procession of people came to visit. A hospital volunteer came to comfort the family. She poured out her story of divorce, remarriage, and a feeling of estrangement from God. But, she added, she now had a desire to renew her relationship with God.

Another health-care professional who was caring for Mandy, uncharacteristically broke into tears. She told of growing up in a boarding school, away from her missionary parents, and never being openly angry with them but never feeling close to them or to God. Now, after caring for Mandy, she longed to regain intimacy with her earthly and heavenly father.

Mandy died that evening at seven o' clock.

Themes: Grief, Hospitals, Love – of others, Parents, Relationships, Suffering.

Scriptures: Matthew 5:4; Luke 10:27; 1 Corinthians 13; 2 Corinthians 1:3–11; 11:30; 12:9; Philippians 4:13; 1 Peter 4:13.

71: Gratitude

Mother Teresa told a moving story about a six-year-old orphan boy. The Sisters had rescued him from the streets of Calcutta where he was dying of fever and nursed him back to health. On the day that he was to leave for another home they gave him a small packet of sugar – a highly-prized commodity among the poor. A quarter of sugar equals a day's wages. As the little boy walked through the gates he saw the Sisters carrying in another child, obviously in great need. He walked straight over to them and handed the sugar to the Sisters, saying that he wanted the sick boy to have it. Mother Teresa asked him why he had done it. 'I think that it is what Jesus would have done,' he replied.

Themes: Generosity, Gifts, Offerings, Sacrifice.

Scriptures: Psalm 112:9; Isaiah 55:10–11; Mark 10:17–31; 12:41–44; Luke 19:1–10; 2 Corinthians 8 and 9; 1 Timothy 6:17–19; Hebrews 13:5.

72: Gratitude

Mother Teresa tells of a man who had been beaten up and was picked up on the streets of Melbourne. He was an alcoholic who had been in that state for years and the Sisters took him to their Home of Compassion. From the way they touched him and the way they took care of him, suddenly it was clear to him 'God loves me!' He left the Home and never touched alcohol again, but went back to his family, his children and his job. Afterwards, when he got his first salary, he came to the Sisters and gave them the money saying, 'I want you to be for others the love of God, as you have been to me.'

Theme: Alcoholism, Generosity, God's love, Love – changed by, Reformed.

Scriptures: Psalm 112:9; Isaiah 55:10–11; Mark 10:17–31; 12:41–44; Luke 10:27; 19:1–10; 1 Corinthians 13; 2 Corinthians 8 and 9; 1 Timothy 6:17–19; Hebrews 13:5.

73: Guidance

In 1979 Khun Paot was nineteen. With 100 others she escaped the Khmer Rouge rule in Kampuchea. They walked through miles of jungles, canals, mountains and rivers. In the end, standing between them and freedom, were communist soldiers and a valley of jungle thick with thorns. Most of the escapees were barefoot or wore flimsy thongs. Intense darkness hampered the struggling group. Paot said they could see absolutely nothing. They did not even know where to step. Suddenly, hundreds of fireflies swarmed into view. The glow made enough light for the people to find their way to freedom.

After Paot was transferred to a refugee camp, she was invited to a Christian meeting. There she saw a framed print of Jesus on the wall. It was the first time she had seen a picture of him, but she pointed to it and said, 'I know that man. He is the one who led us and showed us the way to Thailand and freedom.'

Themes: God – his care, Miracles.

Scriptures: Exodus 13:21–22; Deuteronomy 31:6, 8; Psalm 23:4; 25:9; 32:8; 48:14; 66:12; 138:7; Proverbs 3:5–6; Isaiah 43:2; Daniel 3:25, 28.

74: *Guidance*

Hannah Whitall Smith, the Quaker lady, tells of a woman who, each morning, having consecrated the day to the Lord as soon as she woke, 'would then ask him whether she was to get up or not,' and would not stir until 'the voice' told her to dress. As she put on each article she asked the Lord whether she was to put it on.

Themes: Faith, God – in control, Neurosis, Responsibility, Trust.

Scriptures: Exodus 13:21–22; Deuteronomy 31:6, 8; Psalm 23:4; 32:8; 37:3–5; 48:14; 66:12; 138:7; Proverbs 3:5–6; Isaiah 43:2; Daniel 3:25, 238; Mark 11:22–24; Luke 7:1–10; John 20:24–29; Hebrews 11:1–3.

75: *Guidance*

Kenneth McAll, in his prewar days as a missionary doctor in China, was walking towards a desert village. He had already had one narrow escape when arrested and tried by the invading Japanese. As he walked, a man joined him and asked him to change direction and go to a different village. He turned and accompanied the man to their destination. When they arrived, the villagers were delighted and said they needed plenty of help. 'But why did you change direction?' they asked. 'You were walking towards a village which we think is occupied by the Japanese.' They said they had watched him walking in the desert, but had seen no man stop and talk to him. When Kenneth looked around there was no trace of the man. It was then that he realised that his guide had spoken to him in English!

Themes: Angels, Miracles, Visions.

Scriptures: Exodus 13:12–22; Deuteronomy 31:6, 8; Psalms 23:4; 25:9; 32:8; 48:14; 66:12; 138:7; Proverbs 3:5–6; Isaiah 43:2; Daniel 3:25, 28.

76: *Guidance*

Alongside the road, just opposite the Empress market in Karachi, sits a fortune-teller plying his trade among the passing pedestrians. In a cage at his side is a small parrot called a *tota*. Spread out in front of him are thirty envelopes. Whenever a customer calls on this man, he will have the trained *tota* come out and, after walking among the thirty envelopes 'thinking' for a while, the bird will pick up an envelope and the contents will guide him in telling his customer how to live his life.

Themes: Faith, God – in control, Prayer, Responsibility, Trust.

Scriptures: Exodus 13:21–22; Deuteronomy 31:6, 8; Psalms 23:4; 32:8; 37:3–5; 48:14; 66:12; 138:7; Proverbs 3:5–6; Isaiah 43:2; Daniel 3:25, 28; Mark 11:22–24; Luke 7:1–10; John 20:24–29; Hebrews 11:1–3.

77: *Guilt*

In September 1895, the White House received this letter from a child.

> To His Majesty President Cleveland
> Dear President
> I am in a dreadful state of mind, and I thought I would write and tell you all. About two years ago – as near as I can remember it is two years ago – I used two postage stamps that had been used before on letters, perhaps more than two stamps, but I can only remember of doing it twice. I did not realize what I had done until lately. My mind is constantly turned on that subject, and I think of it night and day. Now, dear President, will you please forgive me, and I promise you I will never do it again. Enclosed find [the] cost of three stamps, and please forgive me, for I was thirteen years old, for I am heartily sorry for what I have done.
> From one of your subjects.

Themes: Confession, Forgiveness, Healing of emotions, Justice, Law, Murder, Pardon, Remorse, Repentance, Sin.

Scriptures: Exodus 20:13; Deuteronomy 5:17; Psalms 31:10; 51; Proverbs 20:9; Matthew 18:21–35; Mark 11:25; John 8:34–36; 1 John 1:8–9.

78: *Guilt*

Edgar Allan Poe tells a story called 'The Tell-Tale Heart'. In it a man killed another and buried him under the floorboards of his home. Soon afterwards he was interrogated by the police. So confident was he of the skilful way he had concealed his crime that he invited the police into the very room where he had hidden the dismembered body. During the questioning, he seated himself in the chair directly over the place of the dead man's burial. But his coolness evaporated as the conversation went on. Soon he sensed a strange pounding noise in his head. But then he realised that it was coming from beneath the floor where the corpse was located. He was convinced that it was the beating of the dead man's heart.

> I talked more fluently, and with a heightened voice. Yet the sound increased – and what could I do? arose and argued about trifles, in a high key and with violent gesticulations; but the noise steadily increased.... Oh God! what *could* I do? I foamed – I raved – I swore! I swung the chair upon which I had been sitting, and grated it upon the boards, but the noise arose over all and continually increased!.... Was it possible they heard not? God! – no, no! They heard! – they suspected they *knew*....

Finally with a shriek he confessed his guilt which was exploding within him. 'I admit the deed! – tear up the planks – here, here! – it is the beating of his hideous heart!'

Themes: Confession, Forgiveness, Healing of emotions, Justice, Law, Murder, Pardon, Remorse, Repentance, Sin.

Scriptures: Exodus 20:13; Deuteronomy 5:17; Psalms 31:10; 51; Proverbs 20:9; Matthew 18:21–35; Mark 11:25; John 8:34–36; 1 John 1:8–9.

79: *Guilt*

In 1992 Jeffrey Dahmer pleaded guilty to murdering fifteen boys and young men. He faced 1,070 years in prison. He was dreadfully aware of what he had done and he knew he deserved to die.

'Your honour, it's over now. This has never been a case to try to get free. I did never want freedom. Frankly, I wanted death for myself. I have seen the tears of the relatives and if I could give my life right now to bring their loved ones back I would do it. I am very sorry. I feel so bad for what I did to those poor families and I understand their rightful hate. My time in prison will be terrible but I deserve whatever I get for what I have done.'

Themes: Confession, Hate, Justice, Law, Murder, Pardon, Remorse, Repentance, Revenge, Sin.

Scriptures: Exodus 20:13; Deuteronomy 5:17; Psalms 31:10; 51; Proverbs 20:9; Matthew 5:43–48; 1 John 1:8–9.

80: *Guilt*

A newspaper reported the tragic story of the drowning of eight-year-old Christopher. He had been accompanied by three friends who said that he had slipped into the pond. They said they thought he was playing a trick on them. It was almost two years before the secret was uncovered when the fifteen-year-old boy who pushed Chris into the water confessed his guilt to a friend. Soon the police were involved.

In those two years one of the three began crying frequently after Chris's death and had to sleep with his mother. A second, an eighteen-year-old, was fired from his job because he would stay home from work on days when he felt angry and disgusted about telling a lie to protect a friend. The third boy started hearing voices and seeing visions and barely talked to his parents. He later entered a hospital for emotionally disturbed children.

Themes: Confession, Forgiveness, Healing of emotions, Justice, Law, Murder, Pardon, Remorse, Repentance, Sin.

Scriptures: Exodus 20:13; Deuteronomy 5:17; Psalms 31:10; 51; Proverbs 20:9; Mark 11:25; John 8:34-36; 1 John 1:8-9.

81: Habits

Raynald III was a fourteenth-century duke of what is now Belgium. He was grossly overweight and called *Crassus*, the Latin for fat.

One day in battle, Edward, his younger brother, captured him and put him in the Nieuwkerk castle. The room was not a cell but a room with a normal door and windows. None of them was locked. But Raynald was too fat to get through the door.

Knowing his weakness, each day his brother sent Raynald a variety of delicious and fattening foods. Instead of dieting so he could get out, he got fatter and fatter. He was a prisoner of his own appetite.

Themes: Dieting, Food, Freedom, Gluttony, Self-control, Sin, Temptation, Weight problems.

Scriptures: Psalms 1; 139:23-24; Matthew 26:41; John 8:31–36; Romans 7:7–25; 1 Corinthians 10:12–14: Galatians 5:16–24; Philippians 4:8; 1 Timothy 2:9, 15; 3:2; 2 Timothy 1:7; Titus 1:8; 2:1–15; James 4:7; 2 Peter 2:9; 3:17.

82: *Healing*

Francis MacNutt is a former Catholic priest and scholar. His book *Healing* is one of the best on the subject. He also has the gift of healing.

MacNutt received a letter from Mrs Sophie Zientarski two weeks after he had prayed for her.

> I am the diabetic over whom you prayed ... and it is with great joy I want to tell you that the Lord has healed me ... [In two weeks] I have taken no medicine, and I feel great. Never in a million years did I think that this would happen to me....

Seven months later, another letter came.

> ... I have the doctor's verification ... and he can't find anything wrong with me.... I am able to do my housework, which last year I could not do. My heart has been healed, too; ... I could not walk up the stairs, and now stairs do not bother me at all. I feel ten years younger, praise the Lord.

Themes: Diabetes, Miracles, Prayer.

Scriptures: Matthew 8:5–13; 9:27–31; Mark 1:29–31, 40–44; 2:1–12; 3:1–6; 5:24–34; 7:31–37; 8:22–26; 10:46–52; Luke 13:10–17; 14:1–6; John 4:46–54; 9:1–34; 11:25–26; James 5:14–15; 1 Peter 1:13.

83: *Healing*

John Wimber tells how he received a phone call from a distraught father. The man was sobbing and could hardly talk. 'My baby is here in the hospital,' he said, 'and they have tubes from machines attached all over her body. The doctors say she will not survive the night. What can you do?' John told him he would come to the hospital. After he put the phone down, he prayed, 'Lord, is this baby supposed to die?' John sensed the Lord saying, 'No!' John walked into the hospital with the knowledge that he was a representative of Christ, a messenger who had a gift for that baby girl.

When John entered the baby's room, he sensed death, so he said quietly, 'Death, get out of here.' It left, and the whole atmosphere of the room changed, as though a weight had been lifted. Then he went over and began praying for the girl. After only a few minutes he knew she was going to be healed, and so did her father. Hope came into his eyes.

'She is going to be OK,' he said, 'I know it.'

Within twenty minutes she improved greatly; several days later she was released, completely healed.

Themes: Death, Deliverance, Demonic, Miracles, Prayer, Sickness.

Scriptures: Matthew 8:5–13; 9:27–31; Mark 1:29–31, 40–44; 2:1–12; 3:1–6; 5:24–34; 7:31–37; 8:22–26; 10:46–52; Luke 13:10–17; 14:1–6; John 4:46–54; 9:1–34; 11:25–26; James 5:14–15; 1 Peter 1:13.

84: Healing

Dr James R. Friend of Bakersfield, California, wrote the following letter to John Wimber.

6 July, 1984
Dear Pastor Wimber...
On Friday night when you were teaching, there was a young mother with her four-and-one-half-year-old baby right down in

the front row. This youngster was terribly brain damaged.... She ... could not feed herself, had never even sucked her thumb, was unable to speak, and her body would go through a constant array of terribly contorted disfiguring, purposeless movements.... Her arms and legs were rigidly spastic, her eyes were usually back in her head and she could not hold her head even for a moment. That night God clearly spoke to me and four other people in that audience that he wanted to heal her.

The child's name is Tina. The following Wednesday we gathered with Tina's family.... The five of us clearly could witness to the fact that God had unmistakably spoken to us that he was going to heal Tina, and so we just laid claim to that in Jesus' name and to the glory of the Father. That began a whole series of miraculous events. First of all ... the purposeless movements ceased within three weeks. The rigidity of her arms and legs began to diminish ... and within four or five weeks she no longer drooled and her eye movement was nearly normal and she was very attentive to those around her. She now sucks her thumb.... She goes to a special school for handicapped, brain-damaged children and the teachers' notes are an accurate chronology of this miracle...

Your brother in Christ,
James R. Friend, MD

Themes: Miracles, Prayer, Sickness.

Scriptures: Matthew 8:5–13; 9:27–31; Mark 1:29–31, 40–44; 2:1–12; 3:1–6; 5:24–34; 7:31–37; 8:22–26; 10:46–52; Luke 13:10–17; 14:1–6; John 4:46–54; 9:1–34; James 5:14–15.

85: Healing

There has been quite a stir in Fuller Theological Seminary over the healings that have taken place in some of the classes.

Sam Sasser had served as a missionary for many years in the

South Pacific. One day he was in the back of the class at Fuller. He was sitting in a wheelchair with his right foot wrapped in a thick bandage. He had survived several accidents, including two in a boat and a plane crash. He also had coral poisoning which had caused his bones to deteriorate. In the prayer time before the class began, Sam asked for prayer. Several students stood around him as someone led in prayer.

The next day Sam said he wanted to give a testimony. 'I don't go for theatrics,' he said, 'but yesterday I didn't mention that I was also legally blind as a result of the coral poisoning. The first day I did not see you as you taught the class. After prayer yesterday, I could see you through the whole class. Not only that, but this morning the nurse came to change the bandage on my foot, and she couldn't believe what she saw. She told me that if whatever had started were to continue, I would be well in a week.'

Within another week, Sam Sasser was walking around the Fuller campus, pushing his own wheelchair. He cancelled his enrolment to learn to use a guide dog. When I heard this story Sam was not able to play tennis or to read, and signs of the underlying coral poisoning flare up from time to time. But God has been greatly glorified as the light of Jesus has brought healing to Sam.

Themes: Blindness, Miracles, Prayer, Sickness.

Scriptures: Matthew 8:5–13; 9:27–31; Mark 1:29–31, 40–44; 2:1–12; 3:1–6; 5:24–34; 7:31–37; 8:22–26; 10:46–52; Luke 13:10–17; 14:1–6; John 4:46–54; 9:1–34; James 5:14–15.

86: Healing

In an interview, John Wimber said:

> I remember one time when a team member and I were called to pray for a woman whose left hand had actually died. I mean, it was black to the elbow; her fingers were drawn up and rotting. An amputation was scheduled for the next day.
>
> The odour was incredible. I could almost see bones through the skin of the fingers. I stood there swallowing, trying to settle my queasy stomach, when suddenly I knew I had to touch that hand. I *had* to.
>
> I put my hand over hers, closed my eyes and prayed. As soon as I got outside the room, I began crying. *Why in the world did I do that? I probably embarrassed her to death by drawing attention to her plight.* . . . We went home with no sense at all of having won a victory or done any mighty deed. I fully expected to hear the next day that the amputation had been completed.
>
> Two weeks later, her brother came up to me with a rather lengthy letter the woman had written – and she was left-handed. It told how overnight her hand had begun to recover just enough to forestall the operation. The doctors kept postponing it a day at a time, until finally she was well.

Themes: Doubt, Laying-on-hands, Miracles, Prayer, Sickness, Touch.

Scriptures: Matthew 8:5–13, 26; 9:27–31; 14:28–31; 14:28–31; Mark 1:29–31, 40–44; 2:1–12; 3:1–6; 5:24–34; 7:31–37; 8:22–26; 10:46–52; Luke 13:10–17; 14:1–6; John 4:46–54; 9:1–34; Hebrews 11; James 5:14–15.

87 Healing

Kate Semmerling tells of her experience as a student nurse in a clinic in Haiti. A woman brought a small boy with crippled legs. He could not stand or walk. She tried to explain that there was nothing she could do, but she wanted to get rid of the woman so, as she says, 'I sighed and offered to pray for her – a God-bless-this-woman type of prayer that would send her on her way.' But there was a grain of faith that told her God could heal, although she expected nothing. She put her hands on the crippled legs and said, 'Dear God, please come and do your work here.'

That was enough faith in that case. Over the next five minutes the legs pumped up as if they were small balloons, and they filled with new muscle. Kate said, 'I thought I was in the Twilight Zone. I had never seen anything like this happen before.' The boy's legs became normal, and he stood up and walked around. Kate's response: 'Oh my God, look at this!'

Themes: Faith, Miracles, Prayer, Trust.

Scriptures: Psalm 37:3–5; Proverbs 3:5–6; Matthew 8:5–13; 9:27–31; Mark 1:29–31, 40–44; 2: 1–12; 3:1–6; 5:24–34; 7:31–37; 8:22–26; 10:46–52; 11:22–24; Luke 7:1–10; 13:10–17; 14:1–6; John 4:46–54; 9:1–34; James 5:14–15.

88: Healing

Susan Speight was a domestic-science teacher in Wetherby. But for four years she had been confined to a wheelchair with a crippling complication of diabetes known as neuropathy. Susan had lost all feeling from her waist downwards. Her specialist had told her that it would not come back.

In June 1977 she went to a festival in Leeds Town Hall where David Watson was speaking. During David's talk one night she began to feel her feet getting hot, and eventually complete feeling was restored. She realised this meant that she ought to be able to walk.

When the meeting was over, she called to Andrew, one of David Watson's team members. She told him what had happened. Andrew helped her out of the wheelchair and together they walked right round the outside of the Town Hall without using her sticks. Realising that she could now walk perfectly, they went back into the Town Hall to tell David and they spent some time together praising God for his unexpected healing power.

Themes: Miracles, Praise.

Scriptures: Psalm 100; Matthew 8:5–13; 9:27–31; Mark 1:29–31, 40–44; 2:1–12; 3:1–6; 5:24–34; 7:31–37; 8:22–26; 10:46–52; Luke 13:10–17; 14:1–6; John 4:46–54; 9:1–34; 1 Thessalonians 5:16–18; Hebrews 13:15; James 5:14–15.

89: Healing

Tony Campolo was speaking at a small college in the American Midwest. As he was finishing his presentation on the second night, a woman came down the aisle of the auditorium carrying her child in her arms. The child was crippled and in calipers. The woman was obviously not a student.

'What do you want?' Campolo asked.

'God told me to come,' she answered. 'You are supposed to heal my child.'

'Dear lady, I don't have the gift of healing.... Teaching is my gift.'

The students had picked up what was going on at the front and there was quite a bit of chatting and sniggering. A very 'with-it' chaplain came to Tony's rescue. Tony explained to the chaplain what the woman wanted. The chaplain spoke to the audience.

'Those who do not believe that this child is going to be healed this evening, please leave the auditorium. If you are not absolutely convinced that this child will have his legs straightened through prayer, I want you to get out of here.'

Five Pentecostal young people were left. They were already 'into it' with their hands in the air and speaking in tongues, expressing their dependence on God.

The Chaplain anointed the child with oil and Campolo prayed. He started with a kind of non-commital, formal prayer. Then he stopped. They all stopped. They felt a strange and awesome presence break loose in their midst. Campolo removed his hand from the child and felt ashamed. They all removed their hands. Tony said that he now expected that the child would be healed then and there. However, it was not. Every one went home.

Three years later Tony Campolo met the mother in another meeting. Standing next to her was a fine lad standing up straight without any calipers. After the meeting, three years previously, the lad had woken crying. His calipers were tight, so the mother loosened them. This happened a number of times over the succeeding few days until the legs were straight.

Themes: Gifts of the Spirit, Miracles, Laying-on-hands, Prayer, Tongues – gift of.

Scriptures: Matthew 8:5–13; 9:27-31; Mark 1:29–31, 40–44; 2:1–12; 3:1–6; 5:24–34; 7:31–37; 8:22–26; 10:46–52; Luke 13:10–17; 14:1–6; John 4:46–54; 9:1–34; James 5:14–15.

90: *Holiness*

Malcolm Muggeridge was a British journalist. He once went to Calcutta to make a film of Mother Teresa called *Something Beautiful for God*. The Home for Dying Destitutes, where Mother Teresa's Missionaries of Charity take down-and-outs from the streets of Calcutta, was formerly a Hindu temple. It has very poor lighting; so poor the cameraman, Ken Macmillan, said it would be quite hopeless to film there. However, he was persuaded to take a few inside shots. When the film was processed, the inside shots were bathed in a wonderful soft light. Ken Macmillan agreed that this could not be accounted for in earthly terms.

Muggeridge said of the incident, 'I have no doubt whatever as to what the explanation is: holiness, an expression of life, is luminous.... The camera had caught this luminosity, without which the film would have come out quite black, as Ken Macmillan proved to himself when he used the same stock in similar circumstances and got no picture at all.'

Themes: Glory of God, God – his holiness.

Scriptures: Exodus 34:29–35; Mark 9:2–3; 2 Corinthians 3:7; 1 Peter 1:13–16.

91: *Holy Spirit*

On 12 October 1492, Rodrigo de Triana was aloft in the rigging of the good ship '*Pinta*'. They were somewhere in the Atlantic. At two in the morning he set up the long awaited cry, '*Tierra*, tierra!' ('Land, land!'). Christopher Columbus went ashore and named the island San Salvador in honour of the

Saviour for answering their prayers.

One of the major reasons why Columbus discovered the New World was because of his courage. It is an interesting feature of the history of maritime exploration that most maritime explorers have fought against the wind and sailed into the wind. They did this because, although they wanted to discover new things, they were more fearful of not being able to go back to where they came from. But Christopher Columbus, a man of great courage, *sailed with the wind*, so keen was he to discover the New World over the horizon.

Themes: Adventure, Courage, Discovery, Faith, Obedience, Risk, Trust.

Scriptures: Psalms 27:14; 37:3–5; Proverbs 3:5–6; Matthew 28:19; Mark 3:14; 6:7; 11:22–24; Luke 7:1–10; 9:1–6; 10:1–20; John 14: 15–24; Acts 5:29; 8:26, 29; 9:10, 15; 10:9–16; 11:1–18; 13:1–4; 15:28; 16:6–10.

Kelty evening Communion 15/4/00

92: *Hospitality*

John Koenig is a New Testament professor in New York. He was once a young chaplain intern at Grady Memorial Hospital in downtown Atlanta in the late 1960s. He writes:

> Entering the duty chaplain's office, I found an elderly black man making himself at home. Seated on one of the two chairs next to the desk, he had propped up his feet on the other. As chaplain on call that Friday night, I had hoped to use this office now and then for a private sanctuary, safe from the chaos of the emergency room and trauma wards. But not now, it seemed.
>
> The man said he was a minister waiting to perform a wedding in the hospital chapel next door. He explained that neither the bride

nor the groom had shown up yet. '*Maybe*', I thought. But how could I know if he was telling the truth? Lots of strange folks wandered about here, especially on the weekends. Just two weeks before, in this same office. I had found myself trying to humour an armed man who was spaced out on drugs. But this man was clearly different, more at ease with himself and with me. We talked, easily from the start, about summer weather and the imponderables of wedding ceremonies, gradually I dropped my guard. 'By the way,' I said, 'I'm John Koenig. I don't think I caught your name.' 'Nice to meet you John,' he responded. 'I'm Martin King.' There was silence for a moment while part of me turned inside out. I thought this man was invading my territory. Now I felt more like a guest than a host.

Themes: Gifts of the Spirit, Humility.

Scriptures: Genesis 18:1–8; Matthew 25:31–46; Luke 18:9–14; John 13:20; Philippians 2:3–11; Hebrews 13:2; 1 Peter 4:9.

93: *Identity*

He began his life with all the classic handicaps and disadvantages. His mother was a powerfully-built, domineering woman who found it difficult to love anyone. She had been married three times, and her second husband divorced her because she beat him up regularly. The father of the child I'm describing was her third husband; he died of a heart attack a few months before the child's birth. As a consequence, the mother had to work long hours from his earliest childhood.

She gave him no affection, no love, no discipline and no training during those early years. She even forbade him to call her at work. Other children had little to do with him, so he was alone most of the time. He was absolutely rejected from his earliest childhood. He was ugly and poor and untrained and unlovable. When he was thirteen years old, a school psychologist commented that he probably didn't even know the meaning of the word 'love'. During adolescence, the girls would have nothing to do with him and he fought with the boys.

Despite a high IQ, he failed academically, and finally dropped out during his third year of high school. He thought he might find a new acceptance in the Marine Corps; they reportedly built men, and he wanted to be one. But his problems went with him. The other marines laughed at him and ridiculed him. He fought back, resisted authority, and was court-martialled and thrown out with an undesirable discharge. So there he was – a young man in his early twenties – absolutely friendless and shipwrecked. He was small and scrawny in stature. He had an adolescent squeak in his voice. He was balding. He had no talent, no skill, no sense of worthiness. He didn't even have a driver's licence.

Once again he thought he could run from his problems, so he went to live in a foreign country. But he was rejected there too. Nothing had changed. While there, he married a girl who herself had been an illegitimate child and brought her back to America with him. Soon she began to develop the same contempt for him that everyone else displayed. She bore him two children, but he never enjoyed the status and respect that a father should have. His marriage continued to crumble. His wife demanded more things that he could not provide. Instead of being his ally against the bitter world, as he hoped, she became his most vicious opponent. She could outfight him, and she learned to bully him. On one occasion, she locked him in the bathroom as punishment. Finally, she forced him to leave.

He tried to make it on his own, but he was terribly lonely. After days of solitude, he went home and literally begged her to take him back. He surrendered all pride; he crawled; he accepted humiliation; he came back on her terms. Despite his meagre salary, he brought her $78 as a gift, asking her to take it and spend it in any way she wished. But she laughed at him. She belittled his feeble attempts to supply the family's needs. She ridiculed his failure. She made fun of his sexual impotency in front of a friend who was there. At one point, he fell on his knees and wept bitterly, as the greater darkness of his private nightmare enveloped him.

Finally, in silence, he pleaded no more. No one wanted him. No one had ever wanted him. He was perhaps the most rejected man of our time. His ego lay shattered in fragments.

The next day, he was a strangely different man. He arose, went to the garage, and took a rifle he had hidden there. He carried it with him to his newly-acquired job at a book-storage building. And, from a window on the third floor of that building, shortly after noon on 22 November 1963, he sent two shells crashing into the head of President John Fitzgerald Kennedy.

Lee Harvey Oswald, the rejected, unlovable failure, killed the man who, more than any other man on earth, embodied all the success, beauty, wealth and family affection which he lacked.

Themes: Love, Marriage, Murder, Parenting, Rejection, Security, Violence – domestic.

Scriptures: Luke 10:27; 1 Corinthians 13; Ephesians 6:1–4; Colossians 3:18–21.

94: *Incarnation*

There is a legend concerning a tribe of Indians who lived around Niagara Falls. Each year the men of the tribe would cast lots to choose a young girl to sacrifice as the bride of the falls.

One particular year the lot fell to the youngest and loveliest daughter of a very old chieftain. He received the news without moving, as he sat in his tent smoking his pipe. The fateful celebration drew near. A little boat was cut out of timber and painted white. On the day, the girl was placed in the canoe surrounded by treasured food. Four men pushed the vessel and girl out into the swirling river as far as they dared. Then they returned to the bank.

As all the people watched the canoe head to the deadly falls they saw another canoe come from the other side of the river. As it got closer they saw that it was the old chief. He was rowing as hard as he could straight for the sacrificial canoe. When he reached his daughter he grabbed hold of the little boat. With one last look of love, they went over the falls together.

Themes: Cross, God – his love, Jesus – his death, Love, Sacrifice.

Scriptures: Matthew 11:25–27; Luke 10:27; John 1:1–5; 5:19–23; Romans 8:32; 1 Corinthians 13; 2 Corinthians 5:19; Colossians 1:15–20; Hebrews 1:3.

95: *Incarnation*

Shah Abbis was a Persian monarch who loved his people very much. To know and understand them better, he would mingle with his subjects in various disguises.

One day he went as a poor man to the public baths, and in a tiny cellar sat beside the fireman who tended the furnace. When it was meal-time the monarch shared his coarse food and talked to his lonely subject as a friend. Again and again he visited and the man grew to love him.

One day the Shah told him he was the monarch, expecting the man to ask for some gift from him. But the fireman sat gazing at his ruler with love and wonder and at last spoke: 'You left your palace and your glory to sit with me in this dark place, to eat of my coarse food, to care whether my heart is glad or sorry. On others you may bestow rich presents, but to me you have given yourself, and it only remains for me to pray that you never withdraw the gift of your friendship.'

Themes: Christmas, Jesus – friend of sinners, God – his Love.

Scriptures: Exodus 33:20; Matthew 11:25–27; Luke 10:27; John 1:1–5, 14, 18; 3:16; 5:19–23; 6:38, 46; 7:29; 8:19, 34–36; Romans 5:8; 8:32; 1 Corinthians 13; 2 Corinthians 4:4; 5:19; Galatians 4:4; Philippians 2:6–8; Colossians 1:15–20; Hebrews 1:3; 2:14; 1 John 4:9.

96: Incarnation

A surgeon stood by the bed of a young woman on whom he had just operated. Her mouth was paralysed and twisted – clownish. A tiny twig of her facial nerve, the one to the muscles of her mouth, had been severed. To remove the tumour in her cheek, the surgeon had to sever the nerve.

'Will my mouth always be like this?' she asked.

'Yes,' said the surgeon, 'it will. It is because the nerve was cut.'

She nodded and was silent.

But her husband, who was standing on the other side of the bed, smiled.

'I like it,' he said. 'It is kind of cute.'

Then he bent down to kiss her crooked mouth. The surgeon watched, moved by the husband's love. As he kissed her, the husband twisted his own lips to accommodate hers, to show her that his loving kiss still worked and that he still loved her.

Themes: Acceptance, Cancer, Forgiveness, Hospitals, Love – sacrificial, Marriage, Reconciliation, Renewal, Sin.

Scriptures: John 1:14; Romans 5:10–11; 2 Corinthians 5:18; Ephesians 2:11–22; Philippians 2:5–11; Hebrews 2:14; 1 John 1:1–3.

97: *Inheritance*

The wealthy English baron, Fitzgerald, had only one son. The son had left home and died while away from home. Fitzgerald never got over the loss of his son, his only heir. As his wealth increased, Fitzgerald continued to invest in paintings by the masters. At his death, his will called for all his paintings to be sold. Because of the quality of the art in the holdings, a message was sent to collectors and museums. A great crowd gathered for what was to be an amazing auction.

When the day of the auction came and the large crowd assembled, the attorney read from the will of Fitzgerald. It instructed that the first painting to be sold was the painting 'of my beloved son'. The painting was from an unknown painter and of poor quality. The only bidder was an old servant who had known the boy and loved him. For a small sum of money he bought it for its sentimental value and the memories it held.

The attorney again read from the will, 'Whoever buys my son gets all. The auction is over.'

Themes: God – his Love, Incarnation, Jesus – his centrality.

Scriptures: Luke 10:27; John 3:36; Romans 8:32; 1 John 2:23; 5:12.

98: *Law*

In Connecticut it is illegal to ride a bicycle at more than 100 kph or carry corpses in a taxi or walk backwards after sunset. In Hollywood it is illegal to drive more than 2,000 sheep down Hollywood Boulevard at any one time. There is a law prohibiting men from stealing after dark in Washington. In Ohio men with hairy chests must wear shirts on the beach. In Utah ladies' heels must not be more than one-and-a-half inches (four centimetres) high. In Virginia there is a law prohibiting ladies from attending a dance without wearing a corset. In Alabama one may not trade mules or live chickens after dark.

Themes: Dancing, Farming, Legalism, Stealing, Sunbathing, Ten Commandments.

Scriptures: Exodus 20:1–17; Deuteronomy 5:1–21; Romans 6:14; 1 Corinthians 9:19–21; Galatians 5:18.

99: *Life*

London Transport's bus-cleaners have to fill in a form if they experience an 'irregularity or occurrence'. One form, filled out by a West-Indian bus-cleaner, reads as follows:

> As I was cleaning from the top floor all my tickets and rubbish, my box is at the top, my feet catch the box and I nok it down and I fell down with it. When the bottom cum, my box noks down my buket.
>
> I go up from the bottom and my brush is at the top and I step on it and I slip and I throw my box to the bottom. I go down to fetch my box and I step on it and slip again as my other foot goes into the buket which has the water and I fall again with my foot in the buket.

I come out of the buket and I fill it with water. I put it on the top stairs and I go down to my box to bring it up and at the top I step over my buket with my foot but it is wet from being in the buket and I fall back down the stairs and I am hurt.

I am going to put water in my buket again wen Mr Chandler say why I am cleaning *his* bus and I hit him with my buket and I am sorry.

Themes: Anger, Christians at work, Humour, Self-control, Suffering.

Scriptures: Matthew 5:22–24; Mark 11:15–19; Acts 16:16–18; Romans 7:7–25; Galatians 5:16–24; 1 Timothy 2:9, 15; 3:2; 2 Timothy 1:7; Titus 1:8; 2:1–15.

100: Life

A newspaper article told of thirty teenagers on death row in the United States. As they wait to die they live in cells four metres by three metres. For just an hour a day they are allowed out for exercise. But even that exercise is solitary. These are young people who have been drinking and on drugs for years. Some of them murdered for money or in domestic fights. Now they are condemned people.

Rather pathetically, Troy Dugar, who killed when he was fifteen and a half says, 'It's horrible here man, it's horrible. I'm planning on going home pretty soon. I'm not going to the death chair. I don't worry about it none because ... my dad's coming to take me home.'

For eight months Troy has been wasting away; the boredom, fear, depression and drugs have eaten away at his brain and personality. His only hope is in the young British lawyer who has dedicated his life to these youngsters to get the death sentence overturned.

Themes: Alcohol, Boredom, Capital punishment, Death sentence, Drugs, Hope, Money, Murder, Prison, Teenagers, Violence – domestic, Youth.

Scriptures: Exodus 20:13; Deuteronomy 5:17; Matthew 5:21–26; Mark 13; John 3:16–21; 11:25–26; Luke 11:1–13; Romans 1:18–32; 1 Corinthians 15:35–58; 1 Thessalonians 4:13-5:11; 1 Peter 1:13.

101: Life

An Israeli housewife's battle with a cockroach landed her husband in hospital with severe burns, a broken pelvis and broken ribs. The wife threw the cockroach in the toilet and sprayed insecticide on it. Her husband tossed a cigarette butt into the bowl, igniting the insecticide and burning his sensitive parts. Then ambulancemen, shaking with laughter at the incident, dropped the stretcher down stairs, further injuring him.

Themes: Emergency, Family life, Humour, Smoking, Tragedy.

Scriptures: Psalms 91; 118:5–6; Luke 8: 22–25.

102: Life – planning

Workmen began drilling for oil in a lake in Louisiana, in the United States. But one day, stunned, they watched a whirlpool suck the 525-hectare lake down into the ground. Nine barges, two oil rigs, five houses and most of a botanical garden went down as well. The geologist did not know that there was a massive salt mine under the lake.

A publicity department ought to know how to promote a product. So General Motors lavishly promoted its 'Nova' car in Latin America. That is, until someone pointed out the ignorance of the publicity department. In Spanish *no va* means, 'It doesn't go'.

Themes: Counting the cost, Second coming, Translation.

Scriptures: Matthew 13:44; Luke 14:25–33; Philippians 3:7.

103: Loneliness

A nineteen-year-old man stood on a ledge seventeen stories above Fifth Avenue in New York. Police and firemen sought to get him to come down, but he shouted to those near him, 'I am a lonely man. I wish someone could convince me life is worth living.' And he jumped.

Themes: God – Love, his, Hope, Suicide.

Scriptures: Psalms 32; 121; Proverbs 18:24; Matthew 10:16–20; Luke 10:27; John 3:16; 10:10; Romans 8:9, 14–17, 26–39; 1 Corinthians 6:19; 13; Hebrews 13:5–6; 1 Peter 1:13; 1 John 4:13.

104: *Love*

A news magazine from America carried the headline: 'I want my son to die,' says mother. The young man was in death row. His mother was so disgusted by the dreadful things he had done that she wrote to the state governor and said, 'Don't reprieve him. What he has done is so bad I want my boy to die.'

He had completed one sentence for rape but when he was released he raped and murdered a teenage girl. He was arrested again and sentenced to death. His name was Jimmy Lee Davis and he was in his early twenties. He was perverted, twisted and rejected even by his mother.

A young pentecostal man in Melbourne read the news article. He thought, 'Jesus loves this man! Oh if he could know Jesus like I know Jesus what a difference it would make.' He wrote a letter to Jimmy in death row and told him that Jesus loved him. He sent the letter to America expecting that the chap would tear the letter up and swear.

To his amazement, within a couple of weeks, he got a letter back saying that, 'It's the most wonderful letter I've ever had in my life. I do wish I could meet you. I just wish I could know Jesus in my life like you do. I've made such a mess of it. You have given me hope.'

Then the young man in Melbourne got the idea that the Lord wanted him to go to America, visit this young man and lead him to Christ. He prayed about it and shared the idea with his friends. Before long all sorts of sums of money were coming in and he had his fare to the United States.

He landed in Jackson, Mississippi, knowing nobody, hoping to get into the death cell to lead this chap to Christ. By a whole series of coincidences he eventually had permission to go into death row, twice a week for four hours a visit, for a couple of months. He took his guitar in with him. He sat in that cell with Jimmy in death row. He sang choruses. They cracked jokes, they laughed, they behaved like brothers.

He led him to Jesus. There was a couple of months of

marvellous Christian fellowship between this young Melbourne pentecostal and Jimmy. The last visit was Jimmy's baptism. A Christian magazine article carried a picture of the prison chaplain and Jimmy dripping with water coming up out of the baptistery. The young Australian's visa had expired and he had to leave. He and Jimmy hugged each other as brothers in Christ.

He came back home to Melbourne and for two years Jimmy waited for his fate. In the meantime, they wrote letters to each other. Jimmy was growing as a Christian and in one of his letters said, 'There is one thing I'm not going to do. I'm not going to dishonour the gospel by using my conversion to escape the death penalty.'

One day the young man in Melbourne was at work when he got a phone call from his wife who said, 'Can you come home at once? Jimmy's just got permission to ring us from prison; he's being executed tonight.'

So he got leave from work and tore home and got through to the prison in America two hours before Jimmy was due in the gas chamber. But he said he just broke down and cried on the phone. However, Jimmy at the other end said, 'I love you man. Thank you for all that you have done for me. I've got to go now. Goodbye. Be seeing you.' And Jimmy hung up.

Themes: Conversion, Love – for others, Self-sacrifice, Testimony.

Scriptures: Luke 10:27; Romans 12:10; 1 Corinthians 13; 1 Thessalonians 4:9; Hebrews 13:1; 2 Peter 1:7; 1 John 3:11–18.

105: Love

Kelty 14/11/99.

The miracle on the River Kwai is one of the most remarkable stories of the Second World War. The conditions for Allied prisoners in the Japanese prisoner-of-war camp on the River Kwai were so abysmal, and the mortality so high, that the men became almost bestial in their selfishness. They did not shrink from stealing food from their dying mates in a desperate attempt to survive. Earnest Gordon, who wrote the book, was himself given up as incurable by the M.O., but was nursed back to life by the devoted self-sacrifice of a man in his Company, Dusty Miller. But the 'miracle' was the transformation of attitudes in that camp as people in it began to understand and respond to the love of Christ. How did that begin to get through to men in such desperate conditions? It all started with a Scotsman, Angus McGilvray, who literally gave his life for his friend. The friend was very ill and about to die. Someone had stolen his blanket. Angus gave him his own. Someone had stolen his food. Angus gave him his own. The result? Angus's friend got better. But Angus collapsed one day from starvation and exhaustion. He pitched on his face and died.

Theme: Atonement, Cross, Crucifixion, Easter, Jesus – his death, Love, Self-sacrifice.

Scriptures: Mark 10:45; Luke 10:27; Romans 5:6–8; 1 Corinthians 5:7; 13; 15:3; 1 Timothy 2:6; Hebrews 9:11–12.

106: *Love*

In a farming village in the south of France there is an annual mid-summer celebration of the Feast of Saint John.

When the first star can be seen in the night sky, the villagers light a bonfire on the school oval. A folk band begins to play and couples dance in a universal two-step, the great fire their only light. It could be a scene from a novel or a film.

At the first break in the music, the couples do not leave for refreshment. They stand staring into the fire. Suddenly, an athletic couple grab each other by the hand. They run, leap high in the air through the flames, landing safely on the other side. As the crowd applauds the couple embraces, glad they have emerged unscathed to dance again. Then another couple try, then another. This leaping is the key to the festival. It works like this.

If you are in love and want to seal your covenant, you make a wish that you will never part, and then you hold hands and jump through the flames. It is said that the hotter the fire and the higher the flames, the longer and closer will be your relationship. It is also said that if you misjudge the fire or one of you lets go and refuses to jump, then your relationship is doomed. So the younger and fitter couples jump early on. This is serious business even though there is much laughter and applause.

At the end of the evening a traditional tune signals a last dance. As the final note on the shepherd's flute fades, the villagers encircle the soft glow of the embers. Then, two old people – the couple married the longest – hold hands, and gracefully, solemnly step over the remaining few coals. They all embrace and walk home in the starry night, all affirming the treasure of marriage.

Themes: Celebration, Commitment, Divorce, Love, Marriage.

Scriptures: Deuteronomy 24:1–5; Matthew 5:27–28, 31–33; Mark 10:2–12; Luke 10:27; 16:18; 1 Corinthians 7:1–16; 13.

107: Love – changed by

In the late 1940s a gunman called Ezio Barberi became notorious in Italy as a cold-blooded killer and the leader of a celebrated gang which raided banks and jewellers, shooting down any who came between them and their loot. He was arrested in 1949, sentenced to fifty-seven years of imprisonment, and committed to the maximum-security wing of the San Vittore prison in Milan.

Although he was universally execrated, this man was loved by one person, a girl of seventeen whom he had never met. Maria Soresina started to keep a scrapbook of Ezio's escapades and crimes. She carried the book around with her and went to church each day to pray for him. She began to write to him regularly in jail. She understood him when nobody else did. She really cared. She pleaded with him. She loved him although he was not in himself the least bit lovable.

Gradually Barberi changed. Being on the receiving end of love like that began to make a new man of him. He had already been involved in organising one mutiny in the prison, but his attitude changed. His violent ways began to disappear. He exchanged the pin-ups on his wall for a picture of Maria. He replied to her letters with a tenderness that he had never shown to anyone or anything before. Was this the hate-filled gangster of Milan?

The new Barberi became a model prisoner. He took a leading part in arranging and carrying out social and charitable events, and worked voluntarily in the prison hospital. Love had challenged him, melted him and won him. And on 18 June 1968, twenty-one years after Maria had fallen in love with him, they were married in the prison chapel.

Themes: Christ's love, Commitment, Conversion, Love – God's, Love – Transforms, Perseverance, Testimony.

Scriptures: Luke 10:27; Romans 5:8; 1 Corinthians 13; 2 Corinthians 5:14; Galatians 2:20; 1 John 4:10, 19.

108: *Love – lack of*

Kathy was about seventeen, her head was shaved, and heavy make-up covered her pretty face. At a Christian meeting she asked the minister, Barry Kissell, to pray for her. She wanted to have a baby. Barry enquired about her husband, but she said she was not married – in fact she didn't have a special boyfriend as she belonged to all the boys in the group. Barry talked to her about Jesus and the wonderful plans which he had for her life which could include marriage and a family. She told him that it sounded good, but she had never meant anything to anybody and wanted a baby so that she could have someone special for herself.

Themes: Hope, Jesus – love of outcast, Lost, Love – God's, Marriage, Parenting, Youth.

Scriptures: Luke 10:27; 15:11–32; John 3:16; Romans 5:8; 1 Corinthians 13; 2 Corinthians 5:14; Galatians 2:20; 1 Peter 1:13; 1 John 4:10, 19.

109: *Love – lack of*

The night before Frank Vitkovic gunned down eight people and plunged eleven storeys to his death in 1987, his family sat around after dinner, quietly watching TV.

A few months previously he had given up his law studies at Melbourne University and had seen the counsellor. No one knew of the hell going on inside Frank's life. That night he retired to his bedroom to write a two-page note to his family explaining he could not go on.

At 4.25 the next afternoon, Frank entered the Australia Post Building in Queen Street. He took the lift to find an old friend and pulled out his gun – a cut-down military weapon – aimed it at his terrified friend and pulled the trigger. When the gun didn't fire, Frank fled. For the next fifteen minutes he went on a killing rampage that put eight people in their graves.

As he gunned down nineteen-year-old Judith Morris he said, 'Nobody loves me.' A few minutes later this unloved man was dead on the pavement below.

Theme: Family life, Killing, Modern life, Murder, Suicide, Violence.

Scriptures: Luke 10:27; 15:11–32; John 3:16; Romans 5:8; 8:31–39; 1 Corinthians 13; 2 Corinthians 5:14; Galatians 2:20; 1 John 4:10, 19.

110: Man

A definition

His symbol: YRU1

Atomic weight: 75 kgs (±25 kgs)

Occurrences: Wherever there are members of the opposite sex – or large quantities of food and drink.

Physical properties: Very active in early development, with great affinity for dirt, grime, etc. In time, displays surface fungus and equalisation of horizontal and vertical dimensions. Hard and brittle on the outside when mature, but still soft as a baby underneath.

Chemical properties: Strong orientation to female species where food not available. Turns to jelly when placed alongside stunning sample of female species. Glows brightly when placed in the limelight but becomes invisible when actually needed. Apparently very complex but very easy to analyse as the way to the heart is through the stomach.

Uses: Hardly any.
Caution: Likely to fall to pieces if dropped, rejected or cut down to size.

Themes: Divorce, Family life, Humour, Marriage, Parenting, Woman.

Scriptures: Ephesians 5:21–6:4; Colossians 3:18–4:1.

111: Marriage

An American surgeon was completely taken up with his work. His interesting career and brilliant success brought him a feeling of full satisfaction. There was only one thing wrong: his wife was very nervous. So he sent her to a psychiatrist.

One day the psychiatrist came and told the surgeon that he was not giving enough attention to his wife. 'You should take her out to a show at least once a week,' he said. The surgeon decided to take his wife out to the cinema every Friday.

A little while later, he met Jesus Christ; he received Christ as master of his life. Immediately he began to listen to his wife in quite a different spirit. He also began to feel responsible for his wife. While he valued the help of the psychiatrist, he knew that sending her to the psychiatrist did not discharge him of his responsibilities. He said this: 'We no longer go to the cinema every Friday evening. We no longer feel the need for that. Instead, we open up to each other, to say all those things we never dreamt of sharing before, in order to discover and to understand each other and to seek God's leading for our home.'

Theme: Divorce, Love, Parenting, Psychiatry, Relationships, Time – use of.

Scriptures: Deuteronomy 24:1–5; Matthew 5:27–29, 31–32; 19:3–12; Mark 10:2–13; Luke 10:27; 1 Corinthians 7:1–11; 13.

112: *Marriage*

There is a story of a young country lass who married a stern farmer years ago. As they were driving back to the farm after the wedding, the horse stumbled.

'That's once,' muttered the taciturn farmer.

A little further on, the horse stumbled again.

'That's twice,' murmured the farmer.

At a creek crossing, the horse stumbled a third time, severely shaking the carriage.

'That's three times,' the farmer growled and he reached under the seat, took out his gun and shot the horse dead on the spot.

The bride protested, 'Darling, don't you think that was a bit drastic? It wasn't the poor horse's fault!'

'That's once,' said the farmer.

Themes: Commitment, Humour, Husbands, Love, Obedience, Sexism, Submission, Violence – domestic, Wives.

Scriptures: Deuteronomy 24:1–5; Matthew 5:27–29, 31–32; 19:3–12; Mark 10:2–13; Luke 10:27; John 14:15–24; Acts 5:29; 1 Corinthians 7:1–11; 13.

113: Marriage

Various historical figures have been used in a promotion for the London Underground. One poster shows Henry VIII with the caption: 'A return to the Tower of London, please.'

To which one wit has added: 'and a single for the wife.'

Themes: Commitment, Humour, Husbands, Love, Wives.

Scriptures: Deuteronomy 24:1–5; Matthew 5:27–29, 31–32; 19:3–12; Mark 10:2–13; Luke 10:27; 1 Corinthians 7:1–11; 13.

114: Martyrdom

In 1956, five missionaries and their families were the first to penetrate the land of the Auca Indians in Ecuador with the good news of Jesus.

In a three-month period, during 'Operation Auca', the missionaries made weekly flights over the tribal area. They made contact with a loud hailer and often lowered a line with a bucket of gifts on the end. It seemed that relations with the Indians below were sufficiently friendly to land on a river bank in their area.

On Tuesday 3 January 1956, Nate Saint and his missionary colleagues landed at what they called 'Palm Beach'. They fished in the river, studied their notebooks of Auca phrases and read *Time* magazine as they waited for the Indians to come out of the jungle.

It was not until Friday at 11:15 am that two women and a man they named 'George' stepped out of the jungle to meet the white missionaries. The missionaries spent the rest of the day showing the Indians such marvels as rubber bands, balloons, hamburgers, lemonade and even a yo-yo. 'George' jumped at the chance to have a ride in the plane.

Towards evening 'George' and the young woman left. The older woman slept by a fire. But she was gone in the morning. The missionaries waited, hoping that they would get an invitation to their village.

Sunday morning Nate took off and flew over the area. It seemed as if the men were on their way to make contact. At 12:30 pm Nate radioed excitedly to his wife Marj, 'Looks like they'll be here for the early afternoon service. Pray for us. This *is* the day! Will contact you next at 4:30.'

So at 4.30 pm, Marj Saint eagerly switched on the radio receiver. There was no sound from Palm Beach. The women waited all night. No sound ever came. The five missionaries had been ambushed and speared to death, and their plane was torn apart.

Themes: Evangelism, Missionaries, Persecution, Sacrifice, Suffering.

Scriptures: Matthew 28:16–20; Mark 6:7–13; Luke 9:1–6; 10:1–20; 24:44–49; Acts 1:8; 4:1–22; 6:8–8:3; 9:23–25; 14:5–6, 19; 16:19–24; 21:30–36; 1 Corinthians 4:11–13; 2 Corinthians 6:4–5; 11:23–28; 1 Thessalonians 2:9; 2 Thessalonians 2:8.

115: Martyrdom

Colin Chapman, in *The Case for Christianity*, quotes Ugandan bishop Festo Kivengere's account of the 1973 execution by firing squad of three men from his diocese:

February 10 began as a sad day for us in Kabale. People were commanded to come to the stadium and witness the execution. Death permeated the atmosphere. A silent crowd of about three thousand was there to watch.

I had permission from the authorities to speak to the men before they died, and two of my fellow ministers were with me.

They brought the men in a truck and unloaded them. They were handcuffed and their feet were chained. The firing squad stood to attention. As we walked into the centre of the stadium, I was wondering what to say. How do you give the gospel to doomed men who are probably seething with rage?

We approached them from behind, and as they turned to look at us, what a sight! Their faces were all alight with an unmistakable glow and radiance. Before we could say anything, one of them burst out:

'Bishop, thank you for coming! I wanted to tell you. The day I was arrested, in my prison cell, I asked the Lord Jesus to come into my heart. He came in and forgave me all my sins! Heaven is now open, and there is nothing between me and my God! Please tell my wife and children that I am going to be with Jesus. Ask them to accept him into their lives as I did.'

The other two men told similar stories, excitedly raising their hands, which rattled their handcuffs.

I felt that what I needed to do was talk to the soldiers, not to the condemned. So I translated what the men had said into a language the soldiers understood. The military men were standing there with guns cocked and bewilderment on their faces. They were so dumbfounded that they forgot to put the hoods over the men's faces.

The three men faced the firing squad standing close together. They looked toward the people and began to wave, handcuffs and all. The people waved back. Then shots were fired and they were with Jesus.

We stood in front of them, our own hearts throbbing with joy, mingled with tears. It was a day never to be forgotten. Though dead, the men spoke loudly to all of Kigezi District and beyond, so that there was an upsurge of life in Christ, which challenges death and defeats it.

The next Sunday, I was preaching to a huge crowd in the

hometown of one of the executed men. Again, the smell of death was over the congregation. But when I gave them the testimony of their man, and how he died, there erupted a great song of praise to Jesus! Many turned to the Lord there.

Themes: Capital punishment, Conversion, Death, Encouragement, Forgiveness, Hanging, Heaven, Joy, Murder, Persecution, Sacrifice, Suffering, Testimony.

Scriptures: Mark 11:25; Luke 10:20; John 11:25–26; 15:11; Acts 4:1–22; 6:8–8:3; 9:23–25; 14:5–6, 19; 16:24–29; 21:30–36; 1 Corinthians 4:11–13; 2 Corinthians 6:4–5; 11:23–28; 1 Thessalonians 2:9; 2 Thessalonians 3:8.

116: Martyrdom

On Wednesday 16 October 1555, all Oxford was gathered 'in the ditch over against Balliol College' to watch the execution of two bishops who had rejected the Pope's authority.

When all was ready, the two bishops were led from their places of confinement; fifty-five-year-old Nicholas Ridley from the mayor's house and eighty-year-old Hugh Latimer from the bailiff's. When they met they embraced each other. Ridley encouraged Latimer: 'Be of good heart, brother, for God will either assuage the fury of the flame or else strengthen us to abide it.' Ridley went to the stake, knelt by it, kissed it and they both prayed kneeling. When they stood they talked to each other.

For fifteen minutes a Mr Smith preached to the crowd on Paul's words: 'Though I give my body to be burnt, and have not love, it profiteth me nothing.'

The two prisoners asked if they could say something, but refrained when they were informed that they could only speak if they recanted their errors.

When they were told to get ready, Ridley gave away to the people around him the things he had on him, including some napkins, nutmegs, his sun-dial and outer clothing. Latimer gave nothing, but very quietly allowed his keeper to pull off his stockings and outer clothing.

The blacksmith chained them to the stake. A bag of gunpowder was tied to each of their necks. A bundle of burning sticks was put at each of their feet. Then Latimer said to Ridley, 'Be of good comfort, Master Ridley, and play the man. We shall this day light such a candle, by God's grace, in England, as I trust shall never be put out.'

Seeing the fire flaming up towards him, Ridley cried out in Latin, 'Into your hand Lord, I commend my spirit. Lord, Lord, receive my spirit,' repeating often the latter part in English.

On the other side of the stake, Latimer was crying out with equal enthusiasm, 'O Father in heaven, receive my soul!' After that he stroked his face with his hand and, as it were, bathed them a little in the fire. He soon died, apparently with very little or no pain.

The younger Ridley lingered for some time in excruciating pain, the fire being choked and burning fiercely beneath, while it could not reach any of his vital organs. At last the flame rose and exploded the gunpowder, and his lifeless body fell over the chain at Latimer's feet.

Themes: Bishops, Death, Courage, Encouragement, Faithfulness, Heresy, Missionaries, Persecution, Sacrifice, Suffering.

Scriptures: Psalm 27:14; Matthew 25:14–30; Mark 11:22–24; Luke 7:1–10; John 11:25–26; Acts 4:1–22; 6:8–8:3; 9:23–25; 14:5–6, 19; 16:19–24; 21:30–36; 1 Corinthians 4:11–13; 13:3; 2 Corinthians 6:4–5; 11:23–28; 1 Thessalonians 2:9; 2 Thessalonians 3:8.

117: *Materialism*

A few miles south east of modern Naples, on 24 August AD 79, Mount Vesuvius exploded. Twenty metres of ash and debris descended and buried the nearby cities of Herculaneum and Pompeii. Seventeen-year-old Pliny, who saw it all said:

> You could hear the shrieks of women, the wailing of infants and the shouting of men; some were calling their parents, others their children or their wives, trying to recognise them by their voices. People bewailed their own fate or that of their relatives, and there were some who prayed for death in their terror. Many besought the aid of the gods, but still more imagined that there were no gods left, and that the universe was plunged into eternal darkness for evermore.

While perhaps 18,000 people escaped, 2,000 people were buried alive in the ash, to be uncovered many years later by archeologists, just as they died.

A rich and healthy upper-class forty-five-year-old woman, whom the archeologists have called the 'Ring Lady', was found where she had been caught fleeing to the wharf to make her escape. She was wearing two gold rings (one set with jasper, the other with carnelian), heavy gold bracelets (in the form of snakes), and gold earrings (probably with pearls).

Not far from her was a lowly helmsman, about the same age as the 'Ring Lady'. He was poor and the fused six vertebrae in his back are signs of a life of strain from heavy manual labour.

Neither wealth nor poverty saved these people from death.

Themes: Death, Fear, Natural disasters, Poverty, Second Coming, Wealth.

Scriptures: Psalms 34:4; 91; 118:5–6; Matthew 6:19–21, 24–34; 10:28; Mark 10:17–31; 13; Luke 8:22–25; 12:5; 19:1–10; John 11:25–26; 1 Timothy 6:10; 2 Timothy 1:7; Hebrews 13:5–6.

118: Ministers

A great method for getting the right minister to help a church to grow is contained in 'The Ultimate Chain Letter' for parishes:

> If you are unhappy with your vicar, simply have your parish secretary send a copy of this letter to six other churches who are tired of their vicar. Then bundle up your vicar and send him to the church on the top of the list in this letter. Within a week you will receive 16,435 vicars and one of them should be all right. Have faith in this chain letter for vicars. Do not break the chain. One church did and got their old vicar back.

Themes: Clergy, Criticism, Discouragement, Encouragement, Leadership, Pastors.

Scriptures: Psalms 23; 42:6–11; 55:22; Matthew 5:11–12; Acts 6:1–6; 1 Corinthians 9:1–23; 2 Corinthians 4:8–18; 10:1–13:10; Philippians 4:4–7; 1 Timothy 2:2; 3:1–13.

119: Miracles

We will call him John. He is only four, but he has a car – a little red one that is peddle-powered. John lives near the railway that goes through the town.

One day John was keen to take his car across the other side of the railway track and try it out on the big stretch of clay there. From the window his mother watched everything. All was going well until John found that the ground clearance on his motor was not quite enough to make it across the line. He got stuck on the tracks. His mother was frantic because she could see that a train was coming. However, she had no chance of getting to her son in time.

But the train stopped! It stopped not far from where John was still sobbing and trying to tug his little car off the line. The train driver had been taken seriously and suddenly ill. He had released the pressure on the automatic control lever and the train automatically came to a stop.

Themes: God's care, God's sovereignty, Parenting.

Scriptures: Daniel 4:35; Acts 8:26–40; 9:10–19.

120: Missed the point

In North Carolina, on 17 December 1908, Orville and Wilbur Wright made the first powered and controlled aeroplane flights. They were so excited that they sent a telegram to their sister Katherine: 'We have actually flown 120 feet. Will be home for Christmas.'

Katherine rushed to the city newspaper office and thrust the cable into the hand of the editor. He read it, smiled and said: 'Well, well! How nice. The boys will be home for Christmas!'

He had missed what could have been, for him, the news scoop of the century.

Themes: Christmas, Opportunities missed.

Scriptures: Mark 2:6–12; 4:1–20; 6:1–6; Luke 15:25–32; John 1:11–12.

121: Modelling

When my daughter was two years old, she was fascinated the first time she watched me shave in the morning. She stood captivated as I soaped my face and began using the razor. That should have been my first clue that something was up. The following morning, Shirley came into the bathroom to find our dachshund, Siggie, sitting in his favourite spot on the furry lid of the toilet seat. Danae had covered his head with lather and was systematically shaving the hair from his shiny skull! Shirley screamed, 'Danae!' which sent Siggie and his young barber scurrying for safety. It was a strange sight to see the frightened dog with nothing but ears sticking up on top of his bald head.

Themes: Families, Humour, God – in Jesus, Jesus – obedient to God, Parenting, Pets.

Scriptures: John 3:11; 5:19; 8:28; 12:49; 14:10; 1 John 1:1–4.

122: Money

John Wesley was preaching on Christian giving and there was a farmer in the congregation. John made his first point: 'Make all you can.' The farmer turned to the person sitting next to him and nodded approval.

Then came the second point of the sermon: 'Save all you can.' The farmer turned and gave another nod of approval to his friend.

Wesley's third point was: 'Give all you can.' The farmer frowned and turned to the friend and said, 'Now he has spoiled it.'

Themes: Giving, God – his provision, Offerings, Money, Tithing.

Scriptures: Psalm 112:9; Isaiah 55:10; Mark 10:17–31; 12:41–44; Luke 19:1–10; 2 Corinthians 8 and 9.

123: *Money*

A pillar of orange fire and billows of black smoke poured into the night sky of Austin, Texas, as firemen arrived at a blazing two-storey apartment building. While the fire engines wailed to a halt, people dressed in pyjamas, underwear and even bedsheets ran from the building. A young fireman looked up in horror as a pregnant girl stood screaming inside a second-storey window. Then, responding to urgent cries in Spanish from a young man already on the ground, she jumped, landing with a thud and a whimper.

The firemen hurried to connect their hoses and advance into the searing heat, but experience told them it was too late to save the building or anyone trapped in it. It was an explosive fire, probably started from kerosene or some other flammable substance.

On the ground, a woman and a man came stumbling out as walking torches. Paramedics ran to cover them with blankets, smothering the flames, trying to comfort them and gently helping them to the ambulances.

'No, no I can't go!' screamed the woman, her face charred and streaked with tears, 'My baby is in there! I've got to get her out.'

But by then their apartment looked like the inside of a furnace. Sadly, a young medic shook his head, and firmly urged the woman towards the ambulance.

It was almost morning before they found the remains of a fifteen-month-old girl in the smoking ruin. But before they found the baby's body, the authorities had learned the horrible truth about the cause of the fire.

A man, angry because someone would not repay him $8, had shot a flare gun into the building through a window, igniting some flammable substance. A building was burned to the ground, 48 people were homeless, seven people were hospitalised and a baby was dead – all because of an argument over $8.

Themes: Anger, Greed, Materialism, Tragedy, Wealth.

Scriptures: 1 Samuel 2:29; Job 20:20; Psalms 4:4; 10:3; 57:4; 91; 118: 5–6; Proverbs 15:1, 27; 28:25; Jeremiah 6:13; 8:10; 22:17; Ezekiel 16:27; Hosea 4:8; Habakkuk 2:5; Matthew 5:21–24; 6:19–21, 24–34; Luke 8:22–25; 12:15–31; Romans 12:17–21; 1 Corinthians 5:9–11; 6:10; 2 Corinthians 8; 9; Ephesians 4:19, 26–32; 6:4; Colossians 3:8; 1 Thessalonians 2:5; 1 Timothy 2:8; 6:10; Titus 1:7; James 1:19–21; 2 Peter 2:3, 14.

124: Money

Roosevelt was once the police commissioner of New York. He was examining an Irish applicant for the police force and asked, 'Well, if a mob was together and you were asked to disperse it, what would you do?'

'Easy,' replied Pat, 'I'd pass around the hat for a collection, sir.'

Themes: Generosity, Giving, God – his provision, Humour, Money, Offerings, Tithing.

Scriptures: Psalm 112:9; Isaiah 55:10; Matthew 6:19–21, 24–34; Mark 10:17–31; 12:41–44; Luke 19:1–10; 2 Corinthians 8 and 9.

125: New life

A vase was found closely sealed in a mummy pit in Egypt by the English traveller Wilkinson. He sent it to the British Museum. But the librarian had the misfortune to drop it and break it. From the ruins he gathered a few peas. They were old, wrinkled and as hard as stones. The peas were planted carefully under a glass on 4 June 1844. At the end of thirty days they had sprouted and were growing well. They had been buried as dead, for about 3,000 years, yet were brought to life by the librarian.

Themes: Death, Resurrection, Submission, Surrender, Water.

Scriptures: Mark 4:1–20, 30–32; John 12:24; 1 Corinthians 15:35–50.

126: Obedience

During the First World War, a French gunner was directed by his commanding officer to train his gun on a little house in the distance in which he suspected the enemy might be hiding. The soldier obeyed and the little house was blown to bits. Highly pleased with the expert marksmanship, the commander turned to his gunner with a compliment, only to find tears rolling from his eyes. Asked why he wept, the soldier said, 'That was my house.'

'If you had told me,' said the officer, 'I might have modified the order.'

'A soldier's first duty is to obey orders,' came the swift reply.

Themes: Following, Leadership, War.

Scriptures: Genesis 22:18; 1 Samuel 15:22; Jeremiah 7:22–23; John 6:29; 14:15–24; Acts 5:29; 6:7; Romans 6.17; 9:31–10:3, 16; 12:1–2; Philippians 2:5–8; Ephesians 4:32–5:2; Hebrews 5:9; 11: 8, 17; 2 Thessalonians 1:8; 1 Peter 1:15–16; 22; 2:8; 3:1; 4:17; 1 John 3:23.

127 *Opportunities – missed*

In the autumn of 1775, a man dressed like a farmer sought lodging in Baltimore's largest hotel. But the manager turned him away because of his appearance. The manager thought that he would bring discredit to his establishment. The stranger left and took a room elsewhere. Later the manager learnt that he had turned away Thomas Jefferson who was then Vice President of the United States. Immediately the manager sent word to apologise to Jefferson and invite him to return and be his guest. But Jefferson replied to the manager, 'Tell him I have already engaged a room. I value his good intention highly, but if he has no place for a dirty American farmer, he has none for the Vice President of the United States.'

Themes: Forgiveness, Incarnation, Love, Peace, Reconciliation.

Scriptures: Genesis 18:19; Matthew 5:43–48; Mark 6:1–6; Luke 10:27; 11:1–13; John 1:10–11; 10:10; 14:1–4; 1 Corinthians 13; 2 Corinthians 1:3–4; James 2:1–13.

128: Opportunities – missed

A family in the very fashionable community of Hillsborough, California, set out to sing some carols for their neighbours. At the very first house where they called, the response was less than the best. A very distraught woman came to the door.

'Look fella,' she shouted, 'I'm too busy. The plumbing's on the blink. I can't get anyone to fix it, and there is a mob coming for dinner. If you really feel like singing carols, come back about nine o'clock, OK?'

'Yes, ma'am,' and, respectfully, Bing Crosby moved his singing troupe along.

Themes: Carols, Christmas, Rejection, Time – use of.

Scriptures: Mark 2:6–12; 4:1–20; 6:1–6; Luke 15:25–32; John 1:11–12.

129: Parable –Prodigal Son

Feeling footloose and frisky, a feather-brained fellow forced his fond father to fork over the farthings.
He flew far to foreign fields,
And frittered his fortune feasting fabulously with faithless friends.

Fleeced by his fellows in folly, and facing famine, he found himself a feed-flinger in a filthy farmyard. Fairly famishing, he fain would have filled his frame with foraged food from fodder fragments.

'Fooey! My father's flunkies fare far finer!' The frazzled fugitive forlornly fumbled frankly facing facts.
Frustrated by failure, and filled with foreboding,
He fled forthwith to his family.

Falling at his father's feet, he forlornly fumbled, 'Father, I've flunked, and fruitlessly forfeited family fellowship favour.'
The far-sighted father, forestalling further flinching,
Frantically flagged the flunkies, 'Fetch a fatling from the flock and fix a feast!'

The fugitive's fault-finding brother frowned
On this fickle forgiveness of former folderol.
But the faithful father figured,
'Filial fidelity is fine, but the fugitive is found!
Let flags be unfurled! Let fanfares flare!'

His father's forgiveness formed the foundation
For the former fugitive's future fortitude.

Themes: Acceptance, Celebration, Failure, Forgiveness, God – as Father, God's love, Humour, Jealousy, Materialism, Parenting, Reconciliation, Repentance.

Scriptures: Exodus 34:6–7; Psalms 51; 103:12; Isaiah 38:17; 43:25; Daniel 9:9; Micah 7:19; Mark 2:1–12; 11:25; Luke 4:18; 10:27; 15:11–32; John 8:1–11; Romans 3:21–31; 1 Corinthians 13; 2 Corinthians 12:7–10; 1 John 1:8–9.

130: Pardon

Queen Victoria was only eighteen when she succeeded to the throne of England. Soon afterwards the Lord Chamberlain presented her with several documents that required her signature. Among them was a paper concerning a man who had committed a serious crime. He had been sentenced to death. The Queen's signature was required for his execution to be carried out. But the young Queen was hesitant.

'And must I become party to his death?' she asked.

'I fear it is so, unless Your Majesty desires to exercise her royal prerogative of mercy!'

To her delight, Victoria was informed that she had the power to pardon the condemned man. She said, 'As an expression of the spirit in which I desire to rule, I will exercise my royal prerogative!' She wrote the word 'pardoned' on the document and the prisoner was set free.

Themes: Capital punishment, Death sentence, Forgiveness, Freedom, Grace, Mercy, Release.

Scriptures: Exodus 34:6–7; Psalms 51; 103:12; Isaiah 38:17; 43:25; Daniel 9:9; Micah 7:19; Mark 2:1–12; 11:25; Luke 4:18; 15:11–32; John 8:1–11, 31–36; 11:25–26; Romans 3:21–31; 2 Corinthians 12:7–10; 1 John 1:8–9.

131: Pardoned

On 30 October 1821, in a Russian hospital for the poor, a son, Fyodor, was born to the chief medical director. When he grew up Fyodor Dostoyevsky studied to become a military engineer. But he resigned his commission and began writing.

It was not many years before his writing got him into trouble. Early in the morning of 23 April 1849, he was awakened by the rattling of swords. His apartment was ransacked. Books and papers were confiscated and he was arrested and taken away to the headquarters of the secret police. He was soon under lock and key. Conditions were hard. They had to live with the fleas, lice, cockroaches and rats.

An inquiry into the writings of subversives like Dostoyevsky eventually took place. Three hundred people were involved in a report over nine thousand pages long. On 16 November, Dostoyevsky received the following sentence. It read, in part: 'The military court finds the accused Dostoyevsky guilty in that he ... accepted a copy of a subversive letter ....Therefore, the military court has ... condemned the former ... Lieutenant ... to ... death by firing squad.'

Early on the cold overcast morning of 22 December, with snow falling intermittently, he was brought his clothes and with twenty others – put into a carriage. When the prisoners emerged from the carriage, they were met by a priest in full burial vestments. He was carrying a Bible and a cross. They stumbled along behind him through the snow. There were three thousand silent witnesses, for the most part people on their way to work. The atmosphere was tense.

In the middle of the square was a scaffold covered with black cloth. Three stakes had been placed in the frozen ground, and behind the scaffold was a line of carts – apparently laden with empty coffins.

The prisoners were placed in two lines on the scaffold facing the troops. By some macabre notion the troops had been selected from among Dostoyevsky's own regiment so that he was to be shot by his friends. With rifles loaded the soldiers took aim at the hooded faces. Half a minute of excruciating, terrible suspense passed. Where were the shots?

Suddenly, someone appeared waving a white cloth and the soldiers lowered their rifles. A carriage sped into the square carrying a sealed envelope for the general. The general stepped forward and announced that the Tsar had granted a pardon. Dostoyevsky felt a joy in life rush through him once again. 'I cannot remember a happier day ... As I walked back and forth ... singing the whole time, singing loudly, I was so glad for the life that had been given back to me.'

Themes: Capital punishment, Death sentence, Forgiveness, Freedom, Grace, Mercy, Release.

Scriptures: Exodus 34:6–7; Psalms 51; 103:12; Isaiah 38:17; 43:25; Daniel 9:9; Micah 7:19; Mark 2:1–12; 11:25; Luke 4:18; 15:11–32; John 8:1–11, 31–36; 11:25–26; Romans 3:21–31; 2 Corinthians 12:7–10; 1 John 1:8–9.

132: Parenting

An American couple decided to take a little orphan girl from a refugee camp with the hope of later adopting her. When she arrived at their home, they showed her a neat little room, a wardrobe full of new clean clothes and told her how much they wanted a little girl like her. They promptly introduced the child to daily bathing. Although unaccustomed to it, the child took the vigorous soaping and scrubbing without complaint. After a week of it, she decided maybe she had had enough.

That night, immersed in a tub of hot water with her face and body smothered in suds, she looked up at her new mother and said, 'You folks don't want a little girl. What you want is a duck.'

Themes: Children, Fathers, Humour, Mothers.

Scriptures: Genesis 18:19; Deuteronomy 5:16; 6:4–9; Ephesians 6:1, 4; Colossians 3:20–21.

133: Parents

Simone Lang, an Australian school teacher, was working in India. She met a little boy, Jonathan, who was in a children's home. He was six years old and he and Simone became close.

One day they were sitting in the school playground, talking. Simone asked Jonathan about himself and how long he had been in the home. He told her how his parents left him at the home when he was three years old, but that he had recently received a letter from his parents saying they were coming to visit him on 1 December. He was very excited and told Simone how much he was looking forward to seeing them. The day arrived and he waited all day. But his parents never came. He had tears in his eyes as he spoke to Simone. She was cut right through as he looked up at her and he said, 'I want a real mummy and a real daddy and a real family.' Simone wanted to put him in her back pack and take him home to care for him. Then he said, 'But I've got Jesus.'

There is a person who had nothing. Yet he had everything. He had not been sidetracked. He knew that God was his father and he was listening to him and depending on him. Simone said that not a day goes by when she does not think about the way Jonathan is listening to his heavenly father and is 100% dependent on him.

Themes: Anxiety, Children, Fathers, Humour, Jesus – dependence on him, Mothers, Rejection, Worry.

Scriptures: Genesis 18:19; Deuteronomy 5:16; 6:4–9; Job 38:41; Psalms 46; 55:22; Matthew 6:19–34; Luke 12:24; Ephesians 6:1, 4; Philippians 4:6; Colossians 3:20–21; 1 Peter 5:6–7.

134: *Peace*

A man was fed up with life. He wanted a peaceful life without all the trauma. He wanted to find a place to live that was safe and secure. So in 1980 he began detailed research to find the safest and most peaceful place in the world where he could live. At last, after two years, he found the place. But two months after he had settled into his trouble-free paradise, the Falklands War broke out in his back garden.

Themes: Anxiety, God – dependence him, Life, Living, Paradise, War, Worry.

Scriptures: Psalms 46; 55:22; Matthew 6:19–34; Luke 12:24; John 14:1–4; 16:33; Romans 5:1–5; Philippians 4:6–7; 1 Peter 5:6–7.

135: *Persecution*

Severe persecution came to Korea when it was occupied for a number of years by a neighbouring country. Many of the churches were closed and missionaries told to leave. Christians were imprisoned and some gave their lives for their faith. A small Methodist church, located thirteen miles from my home in the village of Jae-am, was opened up without explanation. Some Christians came joyfully to the church. Then, suddenly, the doors were locked from the outside, petrol was poured around the church and it was set on fire. A squad of police surrounded the building, ready to shoot any who might try to escape through a window. Twenty-nine people died inside the burning building. They died singing the hymn that Korean Christians still love to sing:

Nearer my God to thee, nearer to thee
E'en though it be the cross
Nearer to thee.

After the Second World War, a group of Christians erected a monument and engraved the names of those twenty-nine people who gave their lives for Christ in the church that Sunday. A few years ago, a group of pastors came from the country that had occupied Korea. They visited this village, saw the monument and heard the story behind it. They returned to their home country and raised $25,000. They used this money to erect a church in the place where the old one had burned down. On 27 September 1970, at 3.00 pm, the beautiful church was dedicated. It was my privilege to attend this dedication service. The church was packed out. The group of pastors who had raised the money were there too. As we sang the final hymn, people automatically got up from their seats and embraced one another. They were proving that the past had been forgiven and forgotten.

Themes: Forgiveness, Hate, Joy, Love, Martyrdom, Reconciliation, Sacrifice, Suffering.

Scriptures: Daniel 3:16–18; Matthew 5:13–48; Mark 8:34–38; 11:25; Luke 10:20, 27; John 15:11; Acts 4:1–22; 6:8–8:3; 7:54–8:8; 9:23`–25; 14:5–6, 19; 16:19–24; 21:30–36; 1 Corinthians 4:11–13; 13:3; 2 Corinthians 6:4–5; 11:23–28; 1 Thessalonians 2:9; 2 Thessalonians 3:8.

136: Persistence

Thirty-one-year-old Catherine Pouleau, a French shop assistant, appeared in a court in northern France charged with harassment. The story goes that Catherine had been abandoned by her lover. In the ten days after being deserted by her boyfriend, she made 3,987 phone calls to her rival and old boyfriend.

Themes: Humour, Love, Persistence, Prayer, Relationships, Revenge.

Scriptures: Matthew 5:43–48; Luke 10:27; 11:1–13; 18:1–8; Acts 1:14; 2:42, 46; 6:4; 8:13; Romans 12:12; 13:6; 1 Corinthians 13; Ephesians 6:18; Colossians 4:2; Hebrews 11:27; 12:1–2.

137: Poor

Mother Teresa related that after Mass one morning she spoke to a group of her nuns.

'During the Mass,' she said, 'you saw that the priest touched the body of Christ with great love and tenderness. When you touch the poor today, you too will be touching the body of Christ. Give them that same love and tenderness.'

Several hours later a young nun came to her, her face radiant, 'I have been touching the body of Christ for three hours,' she said. Mother Teresa asked her what she meant.

'Just as we arrived, the sister brought in a man covered with maggots. He had been picked up from a drain. I have been taking care of him, I have been touching Christ. I knew it was him,' she said.

Themes: Good Samaritan, Hunger, Kindness, Love – of stranger, Neighbours, Poverty.

Scriptures: Isaiah 58:1–7; Ezekiel 18:5–9; Psalm 41:1–3; Proverbs 14:21, 31; 17:5; 19:17; Matthew 10:40–42;

25:31–46; Luke 10:25–37; 1 Corinthians 13; 2 Corinthians 9:6–8; Colossians 3:12–13; Hebrews 13:2; James 1:27; 2:14–17.

138: Prayer

In 1938, Alf Stanway had just taken over as principal of an African Christian boarding school on the coast of Kenya. One of the subjects to be taught was tailoring and the only tailors available were Moslems. All Alf's attempts to find a teacher failed.

During the holidays he was at a conference. He was so worried about the lack of a teacher for his school that he could not concentrate on the task in hand. In desperation he asked God to take away the anxiety. What he did not anticipate was that God took away the anxiety so completely that he forgot all about the issue.

Not until Alf returned to the school and was entering the office did he think of the lack of a tailoring teacher again. And school was due to begin in three days! Alf greeted Joseph the clerk and asked what could be done about a tailor. Joseph simply replied that there was one in the workshop. The man in the workshop had heard of the vacancy and came to investigate. Joseph had given him temporary work until Alf had returned from the conference. He was suitable and was given the job.

Themes: Answered prayer, Anxiety, Guidance, Missionaries, Trust, Worry.

Scriptures: Psalms 32:8; 37:3–5; 46; Proverbs 3:5–6; Jeremiah 29:12–13; Matthew 6:19–34; 21:22; Mark 11:24; Luke 11:1–13; 18:1–6; John 15:7; 16:23–24; Philippians 4:6; James 1:5–8; 4:3; 1 Peter 5:6–7; 1 John 3:22; 5:14–15.

139: Prayer

D.L. Moody, the famous American evangelist of the last century, was in England. He was a young man, and his great work hadn't really begun. He was invited to preach in a large London church. In the morning service he sensed nothing memorable, despite large numbers. In the evening the whole atmosphere was different. The church was alive in the Spirit! Scores of people answered his call for commitment. The response was so great that he had to minister for several nights. This, humanly speaking, led to the salvation of thousands. Intrigued, he tried to find out what was the difference between the morning and evening congregations.

Eventually he tracked down a bedridden woman whose sister came to the church. Every Sunday she would ask her sister about the services. Inevitably she would be given a monotonous and uneventful account. One Sunday the sister mentioned to the bed-ridden woman that a Mr Moody from America had preached that morning. 'Ah!' said the bed-ridden woman, 'I will have no lunch. I must pray.' She had once read an article by Mr Moody, and had prayed for *several years* for God to bring him to England to her church. Now her prayer had been answered, and things were going to happen. The results of that prayer were far-reaching for her church, and even more so for the worldwide church – a new spiritual giant was born.

Themes: Conversion, Evangelism, Ministry, Persistence, Preaching.

Scriptures: Jeremiah 29:12–13; Matthew 21:22; Mark 11:24; Luke 11:1–13; 18:1–6; John 15:7; 16:23–24; 17:20–26; Ephesians 6:18–20; Colossians 4:3; 1 Thessalonians 5:25; 2 Thessalonians 3:1; James 1:5–8; 4:3; 1 John 3:22; 5:14–15.

140: Prayer – meditation

A peasant had got into the habit of slipping into a certain church at a certain time of day with clockwork regularity. There, day by day, he would sit and apparently do nothing. The parish priest observed this regular silent visitor. One day, unable to contain his curiosity any longer, he asked the old man why he came to the church, alone, day in, day out. Why waste his time this way?

The old man looked at the priest and, with a loving twinkle in his eye, explained, 'I look at him. He looks at me. And we tell each other that we love each other.'

Themes: Contemplation, Love – for God, Meditation.

Scriptures: Deuteronomy 6:5; 10:12; Joshua 1:8; Psalms 1:3; 18:1; 19:14; 25; 40:1–5; 63:5–8; 77:11–15; 104:34; 116:1–2; 119; 130:5–6; 143:5; Lamentations 3:25; Luke 10:27; John 14:15; 21:15–19; 1 Corinthians 13; 1 John 4:19.

141: Prayer – unanswered

Canon Jim Glennon of Sydney tells his story of prayer for healing in his own life.

Jim says that he was in an eye hospital. The ophthalmic specialist came to examine his eye and, as he bent over Jim, he caught sight of his neck and said, 'My God, do you know what you have got? You have got multiple skin cancer.'

Jim was discharged from the eye hospital and he took time to think about his skin cancer. For he suspected that, as is often the case, a lack of forgiveness can manifest itself in a breakdown in our bodies. He approached the Reverend Tom

Jewett and asked for his help. He took Jim Glennon very much by surprise by saying, 'Can I come to your home for three days?'

'Yes,' said Canon Glennon. 'But whyever do you want to come to my home for three days?'

'We want to clear away the barriers to healing,' was the reply.

What had to be cleared away was lack of forgiveness. As he tells the story, Canon Glennon says that he had a series of arguments and disagreements with another member of the Cathedral staff. He was hurt and resentful and had to resign his position even though the problems had not been his own fault. Jim Glennon chose to do something about it. He wrote to the person, saying that he was sorry for his part in the disagreement. A reply came shortly afterwards. He accepted what Jim had said, saw that it was sincere and wanted to say that he was sorry about his part in the disagreement. In Jim's mind there was a coming together, a forgiveness and a fellowship. He never entertained another resentful thought about him.

Then this is what Jim Glennon says, 'I solemnly record that the skin cancer cleared up of its own accord without any medical intervention and never came back.'

Themes: Cancer, Forgiveness, Healing, Reconciliation, Sickness.

Scriptures: 2 Samuel 11; Psalms 31:9–10; 32; 38; 51; Mark 2:1–12; 11:25; 1 Corinthians 11:29–32.

142: Pride

One day an MG pulled alongside a Rolls Royce at the traffic lights.

'Do you have a car phone?' the driver asked the man in the Rolls.

'Of course I do!'

'Do you have a fax machine?'

'Of course!'

'What about a double bed, do you have one of those in the back of the Rolls?'

There was no reply as the driver of the Rolls sped off. But that afternoon he had a double bed fitted to his car.

A week later, the Rolls driver passed the same MG. It was parked on the side of the road, its windows were all fogged up and there was steam coming out of the gaps.

The Rolls driver banged on the steamy window. Eventually the MG driver opened the door to be told that the Rolls had a double bed. The MG driver was not at all impressed.

'You got me out of the shower to tell me that?'

Themes: Also: Cars, Coveting, Envy, Humour, Jealousy, Materialism.

Scriptures: 1 Kings 20:11; Psalms 5:5; 12:3; 18:27; 101:5–6; Proverbs 11:2; 15:25; 16:18–19; 25:14; Isaiah 2:6–22; 10:12–19; Mark7:22; Luke 18:9; Romans 1:30; 2:23; 11:20; 1 Corinthians 1:25–31; 2 Corinthians 4:1, 5; 6:3–10; 7:14; 8:28; 3:5; 14; 4:16; 1 John 2:15–17.

143: Ransomed

Eric was the grandson of a motor magnate. At 5.00 pm on Wednesday 13 April 1960, four-and-a-half-year-old Eric Peugeot, his seven-year-old brother Jean-Philippe and an eight-year-old girl were playing in a park next to the Saint-Cloud golf course in a fashionable district on the outskirts of Paris. The chauffeur and a nurse were in a car twenty yards away.

As the three children took turns in going down a slide, an ordinary twenty-year-old young man came through an opening in a broken wall, took Eric's hand and said, 'Come along,' just as if they were going for a walk.

The nurse noticed that Eric had gone, rushed to the slide and found a note on the ground. It was typed in red, warning the family not to contact the police and saying that the child would suffer unless the ransom of 50 million old French francs (equivalent to £35,000 or $75,000) was paid.

That night Roland, the father, went on French radio and said, 'My only concern is to get my child back safe and sound.'

The next day the father stood under an archway with the pass words 'keep the key' and was told not to look around as the money was taken and the person's footsteps could be heard retreating. That night a motorist found little Eric crying on a side street in the West End of Paris. There was a wonderfully happy reunion amid much rejoicing. 'I am happy, terribly happy,' said Eric's father at a press conference at his home.

Themes: Atonement, Cross, Expiation, Freedom, Jesus – his work, Rescue, Reconciliation, Redeemed.

Scriptures: Exodus 6:6; Psalm 77:14–15; Mark 10:45; Luke 24:21; John 1:29; 8:31–36; 1 Corinthians 1:30; 5:7; 6:19–20; 7:22–23; Galatians 3:13; 4:4–5; 5:1; Ephesians 1:7; 5:2; Titus 2:14; Hebrews 9:15; 1 Peter 1:18–19; 1 John 2:2.

144: Rejection

Jodie Cadman is the street name of a New Zealand girl who came to live in the eastern states of Australia. At one point in her story she says that she never quite forgot her mother's words which she overheard when she was six. This particular day began like any other in her six-year-old world.

It was the Christmas holidays at the end of her first year at school. She woke to a brisk breeze and bright blue skies, and was soon out playing with Susan and Margie Johnson from next door. Jodie's place had a small backgarden. Their games centred around a large white-flowering tree at the foot of the garden. This particular day was unusually hot.

At one point, Jodie slipped inside for a drink. She was at the fridge when she realized that her mother was talking to Mrs Johnson in the next room. So she had a listen. Suddenly, she heard her name. She crept a little nearer the wall. Her mother was talking.

'I can't bear to touch Jodie. I wish I'd never had a girl. She just revolts me, somehow,' her mother said.

Jodie could not move. In a few seconds, her whole world had changed. She huddled, white-faced and shaking, against the wall, trying not to cry. She hardly heard anything else her mother was saying. There was something about a baby boy that was 'stillborn'. But then there was a shuffle and a rattle of tea cups so she shakily tiptoed outside.

Susan and Margie must have been sick of waiting, for they had gone home. Never mind, Jodie was relieved. She claimed the old tree and cried and cried until there was no more tears. Eventually it got dark and cool.

Jodie went inside to tea. Nobody seemed to notice how quiet Jodie was. The hurt grew inside her like an ulcer and she began to hate both her parents.

'How dare my mother not love me,' she thought. 'She is my mother.'

Jodie noticed more and more that Mum cuddled her brothers

fondly. She craved the same affection and would run up to her mother, but she would be pushed away.

At one stage she says in the book, 'I feel as if I am desperately searching for something and I don't even know what I'm searching for. Maybe it's happiness. Or love, I don't know. ... Nothing satisfies me. I still feel hollow. Frighteningly hollow. There's still something missing. Something important. Perhaps if ever I found it, I'd know what life was all about and what the point was in it all.'

She reached a stage in her life where she wanted God to deal with her feeling of rejection. Friends, Charles and Jill prayed for her. In the praying, Charles said to her, 'God wants you to forgive your mother, Jodie, for everything she did and everything she didn't do.'

Jodie's fists were clenched with the familiar anger. 'Why the hell should I?' she asked. 'She doesn't deserve to be forgiven. She couldn't care whether I forgave her or not.' Charles explained a very important biblical principle. That is, God cannot do much with us unless we are prepared to release our revengeful grip on those who have hurt us. When Jodie released her hate and revengeful grip on her mother she said, 'I felt an enormous weight lift off me.... I felt strangely warm and peaceful inside like I'd never felt before.'

Over a period of time she met a number of Christians who really knew what peace was about. It was not a smooth road for Jodie to discover that peace for herself. But by the end of the book she is saying things like, 'I love being alive.'

The last thing she says in the book is, 'It's just so good being able to live peacefully myself and with other people. I'm at peace with God. The anger's gone out of me. I didn't want to live, most of my life I was running away, searching. I'm glad to be alive now. I just want to thank Jesus for giving me life.'

Themes: Anger, Forgiveness, Grief, Hate, Healing – inner, Lord's Prayer, Love, Mothers, Parenting, Peace, Reconciliation, Revenge, Violence – domestic.

Scriptures: Genesis 18:19; Deuteronomy 5:16; 6:4–9; Matthew 5:4, 22–24, 43–48; 6:5–15; Mark 11:25; Luke 10:27; 11:1–13; John 5:40; 10:10; 14:1–4; 16:33; Romans 5:1–5; 1 Corinthians 13; 2 Corinthians 1:3–4; Ephesians 6:1; Philippians 4:6–7; Colossians 3:20–21.

145: *Rejection*

When a young fellow called Kirk was in his final year at school, he was a straight-A student. Not surprisingly, he got his first preference in what he wanted to do at university.

Kirk is the son every parent wishes they had – except for Kirk's dad. His dad is an alcoholic. To make matters worse, he is verbally abusive during his binges – calling members of the family cruel names. He nags Kirk for every failing he can find in him. He keeps telling Kirk he will never amount to much. Kirk's mum has been so browbeaten into submission that she never says anything in Kirk's defence.

After Kirk had opened the letter that gave him his place at university, he was so excited he almost floated into the kitchen. Then he came face to face with his half-drunk father. Before he could saying anything he was hit with another lot of abuse, 'Kirk I don't like you. In fact I don't love you. You are a loser and you always will be a loser.'

Themes: Alcoholism, Anger, Fathers, Forgiveness, Grief, Hate, Healing – inner, Lord's Prayer, Love, Mothers, Parenting, Peace, Reconciliation, Revenge, Violence – domestic.

Scriptures: Genesis 18:19; Deuteronomy 5:16; 6:4–9; Matthew 5:4, 43–48; 6:5–15; Mark 11:25; Luke 10:27; 11:1–13; John 5:40; 10:10; 14:1–4; Romans 5:1–5;

1 Corinthians 13; 2 Corinthians 1:3–4; Ephesians 6:1; Philippians 4:6–7; Colossians 3:20–21.

146: Representative

The Sawi people live in New Guinea. Until recent years they were headhunting cannibals who used the skulls of their victims as pillows.

In the first two months that Don and Carol Richardson were in the area to tell them about God's love, they saw fourteen inter-village battles within sight of where they lived. This did not include run-of-the-mill quarrels when, for example, a husband would punish his wife by shooting an arrow through her arm or through her leg.

One day a young fellow from one village called a man from another village, just through the trees, 'lizard-skin'. Soon one man was killed and others were terribly wounded. Don pleaded with the fuming men to make peace between the two villages. But the Richardsons got nowhere fast.

That night they decided it was best to leave. Just as Don turned off his lamp there was movement outside their back-door. He took a torch to investigate. A large group of leading men had come to plead with Don not to leave them. The speaker steeled himself as he said, 'Tomorrow we are going to make peace.'

Don and Carol hardly slept that night wondering what was going to happen. Through most of the night they could hear shrill voices. In the morning, apart from animal noises, it was deathly quiet.

Then they saw a man, one of his baby sons clinging passively to his back, climb down from his long-house. His wife was sobbing violently as they walked past the group in the centre of the village. Suddenly she wiped away the tears from her eyes, grabbed the child and ran off screaming. The man ran after her but one of his older sons stopped him. Now other women were clutching their babies, crying out.

Don and Carol had no idea what was going on. Then, out of the corner of his eye, Don noticed Kaiyo slip away from the crowd and climb into his home. Kaiyo looked down on his only child, six-month-old Baikadon, lying on the grass mat. The little fellow waved his arms around in anticipation of being picked up. Kaiyo's heart was near to bursting. But he knew that there would be no peace in the village if he did not act. When his wife saw him leap down from the far end of the long-house and run towards the next village with Baikadon in his arms she tried to run after him. But she could not keep up. She collapsed on the ground in grief, crying out repeatedly, 'Baikadon! Baikadon, my son!'

Kaiyo's chest was heaving as he reached the mass of leading men of the next village. With Baikadon in his arms, he said to one of them, 'Will you plead the words of my village among your people.'

'Yes!' was the reply.

'Then,' said Kaiyo, 'I give you my son and with him my name.' He held out his only son. A leading man received him gently and said, 'It is enough! I will surely plead for peace between us!' Then there was a great roar from the people as the tension and emotion was released in the two once-warring villages.

Another child, this time from the other village, was brought to Kaiyo's village. In a similar way he was handed over. Young and old from the village filed past the new child in their midst and put a hand on it, sealing their acceptance of the peace this child brought. The atmosphere of the villages had been transformed.

Don asked one of the men if such a painful exchange of children was really necessary. He replied, 'You've been urging us to make peace – don't you know it's impossible to have peace without a *peace child*?'

Themes: Atonement, Cross, Jesus – his death, Missionaries, Peace, Reconciliation, Violence, War.

Scriptures: Exodus 6:6; Psalm 77:14–15; Mark 10:45; Luke 15:3–32; 24:21; John 1:29; 14:1–4; 16:33; Romans 5:1–11; 1 Corinthians 1:30; 5:7; 6:19–20; 7:22–23; 2 Corinthians 5:18–20; Galatians 3:13; 4:4–5; 5:1; Ephesians 1:7; 2:11–21; 5:2; Philippians 4:6–7; Colossians 1:19–23; Titus 2:14; James 4:4; Hebrews 9:15; 1 Peter 1:18–19; 1 John 2:2; 4:7–21.

147: Rescued

In March 1991, a Major Lorenzo flew his stolen Soviet-made MiG 23 fighter jet out of Cuba to Florida.

But in December 1992, Lorenzo flew back to Cuba to rescue his family. Once out over the sea he had to fly the *144 kilometres* about *3 metres* above the water to avoid being picked up by the Cuban radar. He landed the four-seater plane on a busy road at a prearranged spot.

Once he got the plane down he faced a number of obstacles. There was a large rock. He had to lift up the left wing to miss it. There was a bus and a truck heading straight for him. Thankfully, they both pulled off the road. The passengers in the bus watched as the plane drew to a stop.

Mrs Lorenzo said to the children, 'It's your dad coming.' She grabbed their hands and started running. Lorenzo opened the door and in jumped his wife and Reyniel, eleven, and Alejandro, six. Then Mrs Lorenzo closed the door and the plane took off to freedom.

At a news conference, Lorenzo was surrounded by his family.

'I am the happiest man in the world because my family is

free,' he said. 'They are my life.'

Themes: Atonement, Christmas, Easter, Evangelism, Family, Freedom, God – his love, Reconciliation, Salvation, Risk.

Scriptures: Luke 10:27; 15:1–7; 8–10; John 3:16; 8:31–36; Romans 5:10–11; 1 Corinthians 13; 2 Corinthians 5:18–20; Ephesians 2:11–21; Colossians 1:19–23; James 4:4.

148: Resurrection See also 'New Life'.

Nikolai Bukharin was a Soviet politician and communist theoretician. For a time, he also edited the newspaper *Pravda*.

In the early 1920s, Bukharin was sent from Moscow to Kiev to address a vast anti-God rally. For one hour he brought to bear all the artillery of argument, abuse and ridicule upon the Christian faith till it seemed as if the whole ancient structure of belief was in ruins. At the end there was silence. Questions were invited. A man rose and asked leave to speak, a priest of the Orthodox Church. He stood beside Bukharin, faced the people and gave them the ancient, liturgical Easter greeting, 'Christ is risen.' Instantly, the whole vast assembly rose to its feet, and the reply came back like the crash of breakers against the cliff: 'He is risen indeed.' There was no reply; there could not be. When all argument is ended, there remains a fact, the total fact of Jesus Christ.

Themes: Communism, Courage, Easter, Persecution, Suffering.

Scriptures: Psalm 27:14; Matthew 28:1–10; Mark 8:34–38; 16:6; Luke 24:1–11; John 20:1–8; Acts 7:54–8:1; 1 Corinthians 15:1–58.

149: *Sacrifice*

Princess Alice was the granddaughter of Queen Victoria. It is said that when William Gladstone was announcing the death of Princess Alice, he told a touching story to the House of Commons in Britain. The little daughter of the Princess was seriously ill with diphtheria. The doctors had told the Princess not to kiss her little daughter and endanger her own life.

Once, when the child was struggling to breathe, the mother, forgetting herself entirely, took her daughter in her arms to comfort her. Gasping and struggling for her life the child said, 'Mamma, kiss me!'

Without thinking of herself, the mother tenderly kissed her daughter. She caught diphtheria and, after a few weeks, died on Saturday 14 December 1878.

Themes: Easter, Grief, Incarnation, Love, Parenting, Sickness.

Scriptures: Matthew 5:4; Luke 10:27; Romans 4:25; 1 Corinthians 5:7; 13; 2 Corinthians 1:3–4; 5:21; Ephesians 5:2; 1 Peter 2:24.

150: *Sacrifice*

Paul Freed was the President of Trans World Radio. When he was in Poland he was introduced to a Christian widow who lived in a simple one-room shack in a dusty village near Warsaw. The lady told how she had been invited to a friend's place to listen to the radio.

She said, 'For the first time in my life I heard of Jesus Christ. My boy and girl listened too. I cannot tell you the joy we all had as we dropped to our knees at the end of the broadcast and found Jesus Christ as our personal Saviour that night.'

As Paul Freed was leaving, the widow touched his arm and asked why there was only one broadcast a week for thirty million Poles who did not know Christ.

'Because we do not have the money,' was the reply.

The woman walked to the corner of the room, pulled an envelope from a crevice in the wall and offered what was obviously all the money she had.

Paul refused it. She looked directly at Paul, and with the dignity of a queen she said, 'Sir, I am not giving it to you, I am giving it to Jesus Christ.'

Themes: Conversion, Evangelism, Generosity, Giving, God – his provision, Joy, Materialism, Money, Offerings, Sacrificial giving, Testimony, Tithing, Wealth.

Scriptures: Psalm 112:9; Isaiah 55:10–11; Mark 10:17–31; 12:41–44; Luke 10:20; 19:1–10; John 15:11; 2 Corinthians 8 and 9; 1 Timothy 6:17–19; Hebrews 13:5.

151: Sacrifice

One day in the summer holidays of 1937, John Griffith, the controller of the great railroad drawbridge across the Mississippi River, took his eight-year-old son, Greg, to work with him. At noon, John put the bridge up to allow ships to pass. He and his son went up onto the observation deck to eat their packed lunches. Time passed quickly.

Suddenly, John was startled by the shrieking of a train whistle in the distance. He looked at his watch – it was 1.07. The Memphis Express, with four hundred passengers, was roaring towards the raised bridge. He leapt from the observation deck and ran back to the control tower.

Just before throwing the master lever he glanced down for any ships below. His eyes caught sight of something that caused his heart to leap and pound in his throat. His eight-year-old son had fallen into the massive gears that operated the bridge. His left leg was caught in the cogs of the two main gears. Desperately John's mind whirled to devise a rescue plan. But there was no way out.

Again, with alarming closeness, the train whistle shrieked in the air. John could hear the clicking of the locomotive wheels over the tracks. John knew what he had to do.

He buried his head in his left arm and pushed the master lever forward. The massive bridge lowered into place just as the Memphis Express began to roar across the river.

When John Griffith lifted his head, his face was smeared with tears. He looked into the passing windows of the train. There were two businessmen casually reading their midday papers. There were finely-dressed ladies in the dining car sipping coffee and children pushing long spoons into their dishes of ice-cream.

No one looked at the control house, and no one looked at the great gear box. With wrenching agony John cried out at the steel train, 'I sacrificed my son for you people! Don't you care?'

Themes: Atonement, Cross, Expiation, Freedom, Grief, Jesus – his work, Love, Rescue, Reconciliation, Redeemed, Substitution, Suffering.

Scriptures: Exodus 6:6; Psalm 77:14–15; Matthew 5:4; Mark 10:45; Luke 10:27; 24:21; John 1:29; 8:31–36; 1 Corinthians 1:30; 5:7; 6:19–20; 7:22–23; 13; 2 Corinthians 1:3–4; Galatians 3:13; 4:4–5; 5:1; Ephesians 1:7; 5:2; Titus 2:14; Hebrews 9:15; 1 Peter 1:18–19; 1 John 2:2.

152: Sacrifice

Legend has it that Hans and Albrecht, two French goldsmiths, wanted to study painting. The only way they could afford to do so was for one of them to work as a blacksmith while the other went to Venice. Later they would change places.

Albrecht went to Venice and over months and years Hans sent money to his friend. At last Albrecht returned home a rich and renowned painter. Now it was his turn to help Hans.

The two men met in joyous reunion, but when Albrecht looked at his friend, his eyes filled with tears as he discovered the full extent of Hans' sacrifice. The years of hard and heavy labour had calloused and bruised his friend's sensitive hands. His fingers would never be able to handle a painter's brush.

In gratitude for the sacrifice, that distinguished artist, Albrecht Dürer, used the work-ridden hands of his friend as models to paint the hands of Jesus.

Themes: Gratitude, Love – of others, Substitution, Suffering.

Scriptures: Exodus 6:6; Psalm 77:14–15; Mark 10:45: Luke 10:27; 24:21; John 1:29; 15:12–17; 1 Corinthians 1:30; 5:7; 6:19–20; 7:22–23; 13; Galatians 3:13; 4:4–5; 5:1; Ephesians 1:7; 5:2; Titus 2:14; Hebrews 9:15; 1 Peter 1:18–19; 1 John 2:2.

153: Sacrifice

In 1952, the Catholic Bishop of Shanghai in China addressed his clergy in these words:

> Fathers, you must no longer entertain any illusory hopes.... You are condemned. There is no emergency exit for you. Once and for

> all, you must now look at prison and death full in the face. That is your lot. That is what God in his loving mercy is reserving for you. What do you fear? You have nothing to lose any more. If we deny our faith we shall disappear, and there will be no resurrection. If we remain faithful, we shall disappear just the same – but there will be a resurrection.

Three years later the Bishop was arrested and imprisoned. After a time he was brought out before a large crowd in a sports stadium. He was dressed and bound as a criminal. For hours patriots came forward and testified against his imperial crimes. Finally this enemy of the people was pushed before the microphone, physically ruined and morally broken. They expected the usual confession. Raising himself very slowly, with a strong firm voice he pronounced one phrase: 'Long live Christ the King.'

Themes: Bishops, Faithfulness, Leaders, Persecution, Prison, Suffering.

Scriptures: Daniel 3:16–18; Matthew 25:14–30; Mark 8:34–38; 11:22–24; Luke 7:1–10; Acts 4:1–22; 6:8–8:3; 7:54–8:8; 9:23–25; 14:5–6, 19; 16:19–24; 21:30–36; 1 Corinthians 4:11–13; 13:3; 2 Corinthians 6:4–5; 11:23–28; 1 Thessalonians 2:9; 2 Thessalonians 3:8.

154: *Sacrifice*

When Richard Wurmbrand was in prison for being a Christian he became seriously ill. He received an illicit gift of two lumps of sugar. He didn't eat the sugar, but passed it on to someone who was in a worse state. Again the sugar wasn't eaten. Apparently it lasted for some two years, passed from one prisoner to another, as a symbol of self-sacrifice and hope.

Themes: Giving, God – his provision, Gratitude, Hope, Love – of others, Offerings, Materialism, Money, Prison, Sacrificial giving, Substitution, Suffering, Tithing, Wealth.

Scriptures: Exodus 6:6; Psalms 77:14–15; 112:9; Isaiah 55:10–11; Mark 10:17–31, 45; 12:41–44; Luke 10:27; 19:1–10; 24:21; John 1:29; 15:12–17; 1 Corinthians 1:30; 5:7; 6:19–20; 7:22–23; 13; 2 Corinthians 8; 9; Galatians 3:13; 4:4–5; 5:1; Ephesians 1:7; 5:2; 1 Timothy 6:17–19; Titus 2:14; Hebrews 9:15; 13:5; 1 Peter 1:18–19; 1 John 2:2.

155: Salvation – desired

Doctor Chamberlain, a missionary in India, says that one day he was preaching about Jesus by the side of the Ganges river. One of the many people who came to bathe in the river was a man who had journeyed wearily a great distance on his knees and elbows. He came to wash away his continual search for life. He dragged himself to the edge of the river and made a prayer to Gunga. Then he crept into the water. A moment later he emerged. There was no elation, only despair as he lay prostrate on the bank. Nothing had changed. But as he lay there he could hear Chamberlain speaking about Jesus. Chamberlain said the man got up on his knees and clapped his hands and said out loud, 'That is what I want! That is what I want!'

Themes: Christmas, Conversion, Despair, Joy, Missionaries, Peace, Religion – others, Searching, Testimony.

Scriptures: Isaiah 9:1–7; Matthew 4:12–17; 28:16–20; Mark 1:14–15; 10:17–31; Luke 4:16–21; 10:20; John 10:10; 14:1–6; 15:11; 16:33; Acts 2:1–42; Philippians 4:6–7.

156: Science

Three scientists at a conference were discussing the most significant scientific advancement in recent times.

The Scotsman thought it was nuclear power for the generation of electricity, modelled in the power station up at Thurso on the north coast of Scotland near the Queen Mother's country home.

The Englishman argued that it was supersonic flight seen in the beautiful birdlike Concorde.

The Irishman's suggestion was that the most significant scientific breakthrough was the vacuum flask. The other two could not believe their ears.

'What is so wonderful about the thermos?' they asked.

'Well, it keeps hot things hot and cold things cold,' said the Irishman.

'So?' inquired the other two.

'Well,' asked the Irishman, 'how does the thermos know the difference?'

Themes: Humour, Salvation – rejected, Salvation – valuable.

Scriptures: Mark 6:1–6; Luke 4:22–30; John 1:11–12; Romans 1:16; 2 Corinthians 4:7.

157: Second Coming

So the story goes, Queen Victoria was out walking one summer afternoon near Balmoral Castle in Scotland.

She wanted a rest and a drink. She passed a couple of houses and knocked on the door of one of them. There was no answer. She knocked a number of times. Still there was no answer. The lady inside was busy and could not be bothered to answer the door. The Queen walked on home.

The neighbour across the road saw all this through her front window. In the evening that day, the two women chatted as they pottered in their gardens. With more than a hint of jealousy, the neighbour said, 'I see that the Queen called at your place today.'

The other lady had no idea and was bitterly disappointed at missing this opportunity of having the Queen to tea. So for the rest of her life that woman waited every day for the Queen to return. She never came.

Themes: Advent, Angels – entertaining unawares; Christmas, Hospitality, Opportunities missed.

Scriptures: Genesis 18:1–8; Matthew 25:31–46; Mark 13:32–37; John 1:11–12; 13:20; 1 Thessalonians 5:1–11; 2 Thessalonians 2:1–11; Hebrews 9:28; 13:2; 1 Peter 4:9; 2 Peter 3:1–13.

158: Second Coming

His parents had gone out and left ten-year-old Michael home with his older sister. She spent the evening in her room reading. Michael could not think of anything to do until he saw the large chiming clock on the mantelpiece over the fire. He took it down. Before he realised what he was doing he had most of the insides out and around him on the floor. He tried hard to remember where everything went and got most of it back in place. However, there were a couple of pieces left over on the floor. It didn't seem to matter as, quite remarkably, the clock went again when he wound it up. But it did not seem to chime on the hour. He hoped his parents would not notice.

Next morning was Sunday and as the family was stirring from sleep the clock in the lounge began to chime. Michael held his breath as the clock struck; one, two, three, four.... nine, ten, eleven, twelve ... thirteen, fourteen, fifteen ... and still the chiming continued. Twenty-seven, twenty-eight, twenty-nine.

Michael was still holding his breath when he heard his mother yell from the bedroom, 'Quick, get up, it's later than it's ever been!'

Themes: Advent, Angels – entertaining unawares, Christmas, Hospitality, Humour, Opportunities missed.

Scriptures: Genesis 18:18–8; Matthew 24:33; 25:31–46; Mark 8:31–9:1; 13:1–37; John 1:11–12; 13:20; Acts 1:17; Romans 13:11–14; 1 Corinthians 7:29; 1 Thessalonians 5:1–11; 2 Thessalonians 2:1–11; Hebrews 9:28; 13:2; James 5:8; 1 Peter 4:7, 9; 2 Peter 3:1–13; Revelation 1:1; 22:7, 10, 12, 20.

159: Service

In 1882 Charles T. Studd was a member of the English cricket team which was beaten by Australia for the first time. Studd was a Christian and was wondering what to do with his life. In October 1884, he said, 'How could I spend the best hours of my life in working for myself and for the honours and pleasures of this world while thousands and thousands of souls are perishing every day without having heard of the Lord Jesus Christ, going down to Christless and hopeless graves?'

He went to a missionary meeting and heard John McCarthy tell of the great need for workers in China. Through this, C.T. became convinced that God was leading him to China. But when he broke the news to his mother she was devastated. She begged him not to go. The whole family went into a kind of gloomy depression. He could not sleep at night with all the conflict and confusion in his mind. On the night of 4 November he was in London standing on King's Cross underground station waiting for the Bayswater train. He took out his little pocket Bible to see what God would say to him through it. He opened it and came across the chilling sentence in Matthew 10:36 – 'a man's worst enemies will be the members of his own family.' He took it that God was indeed calling him to mission work.

C.T. Studd worked in China, in India and then in Africa for a total of over forty years.

Themes: Call, Missionaries, Obedience, Opposition, Parents.

Scriptures: Genesis 12:1–5; Exodus 3:1–22; 1 Samuel 3:1–21; Isaiah 6:1–13; Jeremiah 1:4–10; Matthew 10:1–15; 28:18–20; Mark 6:6–13; Acts 9:1–19; 13:1–3.

160: *Service*

There are 560 members in our church
But 100 are frail and elderly
That leaves 460 to do all the work
But 74 are young people at college
That leaves 386 to do all the work
But 150 are tired businessmen
So that leaves 236 to do all the work
And 150 are housewives with children
That leaves 86
A further 46 have other important interests
That leaves 40 to do all the work
But 15 live too far away to come regularly
So that leaves 25 to do all the work
And 23 say they have done their bit.

So that leaves you and me
And I'm exhausted
Good luck to you.

Themes: Gifts of the Spirit, Laziness, Ministry.

Scriptures: Romans 12:3–8; Corinthians 12:1–14:39; Ephesians 4:11–16; 1 Peter 4:10–11.

161: Sex

Yves of Chartres instructed the devout to abstain from sexual intercourse on Thursdays and Fridays in remembrance of Christ's rapture and crucifixion, on Saturdays to honour the Virgin Mary, on Sundays to commemorate Christ's resurrection, and on Mondays out of respect for departed souls.

Themes: Celibacy, Humour, Legalism, Marriage.

Scriptures: 1 Corinthians 7:1–6.

162: Sex

An ancient Jewish text has these directions for normal sexual relations. For sailors it is twice a year. For camel-drivers it is once a month. For donkey-drivers it is once a week. For labourers it is twice a week. For the unemployed it is every day. There are clearly some benefits for the unemployed!

Themes: Humour, Marriage, Unemployment.

Scriptures: I Corinthians 7:1–6.

163: Sin

I went to my psychiatrist to be psychoanalysed
To find out why I killed the cat and blackened my husband's eyes.
He laid me on a downy couch to see what he could find,
And here is what he dredged up from my subconscious mind:
When I was one, my mommie hid my dollie in a trunk,
And so it follows naturally that I am always drunk.
When I was two, I saw my father kiss the maid one day,
And that is why I suffer now from kleptomania.
At three, I had the feeling of ambivalence toward my brothers,
And so it follows naturally I poison all my lovers.
But I am happy; now I've learned the lesson this has taught;
That everything I do that's wrong is someone else's fault.

Themes: Confession, Forgiveness, Murder, Sin – original, stealing.

Scriptures: Genesis 3:1–24; Mark 11:25; John 8:34–36, 44; Romans 1:18–3:20; 1 Timothy 2:14; James 1:13–15; 2 Peter 2:4; 1 John 3:8; Jude 6.

164: *Slavery*

It is told that once in the days before the ending of slavery, Lincoln bought a slave girl with the sole purpose of giving her her freedom. She did not realise why he was buying her; she thought it was simply another transaction in which she was involved as a thing. So he paid the price for her; and then handed her her papers of freedom. She did not even understand. 'You are free,' he said to her gently. 'Free?' she said. 'Can I go wherever I want to go now?' 'Indeed you can,' he said. 'Then,' she said, 'if I am free to go anywhere I will stay with you and serve you until I die.'

Themes: Atonement, Cross, Expiation, Freedom, Jesus – his work, Redeemed, Rescue.

Scriptures: Exodus 6:6; Psalm 77:14–15; Mark 10:45; Luke 24:21; John 1:29; 8:31–36; 1 Corinthians 1:30; 5:7; 6:19–20; 7:22–23; Galatians 3:13; 4:4–5; 5:1; Ephesians 1:7; 5:2; Titus 2:14; Hebrews 9:15; 1 Peter 1:18–19; 1 John 2:2.

165: *Stress*

Recently, a man in Florida in the United States watched a cash dispenser eat up *two* of his cards. It was obviously the last straw on the wrong day of the week for him. He took out a .32 calibre pistol and fired six rounds into the mouth of the hungry machine.

Themes: Anxiety, Fear, Worry.

Scriptures: Psalms 34:4; 46; 55:22; Matthew 6:19–34; 10:28; Luke 12:5, 22–31; Romans 12:12; Philippians 4:6; 2 Timothy 1:7; Hebrews 13:5–6; 1 Peter 5:6–7.

166: *Stress*

In central London, during the nightly bombing raids of the Second World War, there was a rise of 50% in the incidence of people developing stomach ulcers. However, out in the surrounding suburbs, where people were uncertain whether or not bombs would be dropped on them on any given night, the rate of ulcers soared by a massive 300%.

Themes: Anxiety, Fear, War, Worry.

Scriptures: Psalms 34:4; 46; 55:22; Matthew 6:19–34; 10:28; Luke 12:5, 22–31; Romans 12:12; Philippians 4:6; 2 Timothy 1:7; Hebrews 13:5–6; 1 Peter 5:6–7.

167: *Stress*

One of the most stress-free places on earth to have a job is Antarctica. Most of the time the eight hundred workers are inside and can read and watch videos almost as much as they like. When they go outside the work is not exactly difficult. They count penguins, they chisel ice, they read the weather instruments, they time how many seconds an ear lobe can withstand frostbite.

However, the list of problems related to the absence of stress among Antarctic workers is remarkable. For example, one Australian cook chased a diesel mechanic with a meat axe for three hours before they both got tired, drunk and reconciled – in that order. A Russian scientist is said to have committed murder with an axe after his opponent beat him in a game of chess.

Themes: Anger, Anxiety, Fear, Laziness, Murder, Relationships, Unemployment, Worry.

Scriptures: Psalms 34:4; 46; 55:22; Matthew 5:22–24; 6:19–34; 10:28; Luke 12:5, 22–31; Romans 12:12; Philippians 4:6; 2 Timothy 1:7; Hebrews 13:5–6; 1 Peter 5:6–7.

168: Substitution

(This long story is included in the expectation that it will yield a number of shorter stories.)

In May 1941 Father Maximilian Kolbe was arrested by the Nazis and sent to Auschwitz concentration camp.

At about three in the afternoon, on almost the last day of July, as men were digging gravel outside the camp to be used in building more blocks, the sirens began to wail and shriek. A prisoner was missing.

After work the whole camp stood to attention until being dismissed to go to bed. There was no meal. The next day everyone went to work except for Block 14, which had the missing prisoner. They were again put on the parade-ground to stand to attention all day in the sun. The only break came at noon when they were given their soup ration. Quite a few keeled over and were left as they fell.

It was about seven o'clock at night when Lagerführer Karl Fritsch, Commandant Höss' deputy, and Rapportführer Gerhard Palitsch, head of the dreaded Political Department, inspected the silent rows of men.

Fritsch barked, 'The fugitive has not been found. In reprisal for your comrade's escape, ten of you will die of starvation. Next time, it will be twenty.'

Immediately the selection began. Palitsch and a prisoner–

secretary preceded him, up and down the rows, with pad and pencil to take down the numbers of the condemned. Fritsch meandered slowly to prolong the terror. Then with a gesture, he chose his victims.

After each row was inspected, the order was given: 'Three paces forward.' They moved up, leaving an alley between them and the next row so the arrogant Fritsch could one by one stare each of these hapless souls straight in the face.

Finally the grisly selection was complete. Together the SS officers checked the secretary's list against the numbers on the condemned. As their passion for accuracy occupied them, one of the victims was sobbing, 'My wife and my children!' It was Francis Gajowniczek. The SS ignored him.

Suddenly, there was a movement in the still ranks. A prisoner several rows back had broken out and was pushing his way towards the front. The SS guards watching this Block raised their automatic rifles, while the dogs at their heels tensed for the order to spring. Fritsch and Palitsch reached towards their holsters too.

It was Kolbe. His step was firm, his face peaceful. Angrily the Block capo shouted at him to stop or be shot. Kolbe answered calmly. 'I want to talk to the commander,' and kept on walking while the capo, oddly enough, neither shot nor clubbed him. Then, still at a respectful distance, Kolbe stopped, his cap in his hands. Standing at attention like an officer of some sort himself, he looked Fritsch straight in the eye. 'Herr Kommandant, I wish to make a request please,' he said politely in flawless German.

Survivors would later say it was a miracle that no one shot him. Instead, Fritsch asked, 'What do you want?'

'I want to die in place of this prisoner,' and Kolbe pointed towards the sobbing Gajowniczek. He presented this audacious request without a stammer. Fritsch looked stupefied, irritated. Everyone noted how the German, lord of life and death, suddenly nervous, actually stepped back a pace.

The prisoner explained coolly, as if he were discussing some everyday matter, that the man over there had a family.

'I have no wife or children. Besides, I'm old and not good for anything. He's in better condition,' he added adroitly, playing on the Nazi line that only the fit should live.

'Who are you?' Fritsch croaked.

'A Catholic priest.'

Fritsch was silent. The stunned Block, audience to this drama, expected him in usual Auschwitz fashion to show no mercy but sneer, 'Well, since you're so eager, we'll just let you come along too,' and take both men. Instead, after a moment, the deputy-commander snapped, 'Request granted.' As if he needed to expel some fury, he kicked Gajowniczek, snarling, 'Back to ranks, you.'

Prisoners in ranks are never allowed to speak. Gajowniczek later said, 'I could only try to thank him with my eyes. I was stunned and could hardly grasp what was going on. The immensity of it: I, the condemned, am to live and someone else willingly and voluntarily offers his life for me – a stranger. Is this some dream or reality?'

The Block was dismissed and the order was given for the condemned prisoners to march to the basement bunker. The SS guard had snarled, 'Strip,' while they were still outside the Block. No sense in carrying their garments up the stairs. Then it was in the door of the innocent-looking brick building and descent into the dark, fetid basement where they were shoved into one of the rank-smelling cells.

By some act of God, the prisoner-interpreter who would watch Kolbe's last days came out of Auschwitz alive. Number 1,192, Bruno Borgowiec, a Pole from Silesia, he says:

> The naked victims were in one cell near those [dying in reprisal because] of the two previous escapes. The foul air was horrible, the cell floor cement. There was no furniture whatsoever, except for a bucket for relieving themselves.
>
> You could say Father Kolbe's presence in the bunker was necessary for the others. They were in a frenzy over the thought of

never returning to their homes and families, screaming in despair and cursing. He pacified them and they [began to] resign themselves. With his gift of consolation, he prolonged the lives of the condemned who were usually so psychologically destroyed that they succumbed in just a few days. . . .

[Kolbe was hearing the victims' confessions and preparing them to die.] So they could join him, he prayed aloud. The cell doors were made of oak. Because of the silence and acoustics, the voice of Father Kolbe in prayer was diffused to the other cells, where it could be heard well. These prisoners joined in.

From then on, every day from the cell where these poor souls were joined by the adjoining cells, one heard the recitation of prayers, the rosary and hymns. Father Kolbe led while the others responded as a group. As these fervent prayers and hymns resounded in all corners of the bunker, I had the impression I was in a church.

Once a day the SS men in charge of the penal Block inspected the cells, ordering me to carry away the corpses of those who had died during the night....

Sometimes Father Kolbe's group was so deeply absorbed in prayer that they didn't notice the SS opening the door. It took loud shouts to get their attention. When they saw the cell door was opened, the poor wretches, weeping, would loudly beg for a crust of bread and some water, which they never obtained.

Father Kolbe never asked for anything and he never complained....

I overheard the SS talking about him among themselves. They were admiring his courage and behaviour. One of them said, 'We've never had a priest here like this one. He must be a wholly exceptional man'...

What kind of martyrdom these men were enduring can be imagined from the fact that the urine bucket was always dry. In their dreadful thirst, they must have drunk its contents.

As the prisoners became weaker, the prayers continued, but in whispers. But even during each inspection the others were always found lying on the cement, Father Kolbe was still standing or kneeling, his face serene.

In this way, two weeks went by. The prisoners were dying one after the other, and by this time only four were left, among them

> Father Kolbe, who was still conscious. The SS decided things were taking too long.... One day they sent for the German criminal Block from the hospital to give the prisoners injections of carbolic acid. After the needle prick in the vein of the left arm, you could follow the instant swelling as it moved up the arm towards the chest. When it reached the heart, the victim would fall down dead. Between the injection and death was little more than ten seconds.
>
> When Bock got there, I had to accompany them to the cell. I saw Father Kolbe, with a prayer, himself hold out his arm to the executioner. I couldn't bear it. With the excuse that I had some work to do, I left. But as soon as the SS and their executioner were gone, I returned.
>
> The other naked, begrimed corpses were lying on the floor, their faces betraying signs of their suffering. Father Kolbe was sitting upright, leaning against the far wall. His body was not dirty like the others, but clean and bright. The head was tilted somewhat to one side. His eyes were open. Serene and pure, his face was radiant.

It was 12:50 pm on 14 August 1941, the Vigil of the Assumption. He was forty-seven years old, 'perhaps the brightest and most glittering figure to emerge from the darkness and degradation of the Nazi epoch' (Pope Paul VI).

At a solemn canonisation ceremony on 10 October 1982, in St Peter's Square, Rome, eighty-year-old Francis Gajowniczek, his wife, children and grandchildren, along with twenty-six cardinals, more than three hundred archbishops and bishops as well as one hundred and fifty thousand people were able to thank God for the sacrificial love of Maximilian Kolbe.

Themes: Courage, Cross, Easter, Encouragement, Jesus – his death, Love, Martyrdom, Persecution, Sacrifice, Suffering.

Scriptures: Psalm 27:14; Isaiah 53; Mark 10:45; Luke 10:27; Romans 3:21–25; John 11:50; 1 Corinthians 13; Galatians 3:13; 1 Timothy 2:6; Hebrews 9:28; 1 Peter 2:24.

169: *Substitution*

On a balmy Saturday afternoon in September, pedestrians near New York's famed Carnegie Hall stared in fascination. Towering over them was one of the world's tallest moving objects: a 200–tonne yellow construction crane whose massive boom reached nearly twenty storeys above the street. The crane sat on the rim of an eight-metre-deep excavation where it was to help erect a sixty-eight storey skyscraper.

Tom O'Brien, one of the area's best crane-operators was in the cabin. Tom's immediate task was to lift a huge steel turntable that would form the base of a smaller crane to be erected on top of a construction tower overlooking the yawning building site. In twenty-two years of handling machines like this one, he had seen two overloaded cranes topple. One operator had been crushed to death in his cab; the other had leaped for his life to safety.

Shortly after 3 pm, the five men on the tower radioed that all was ready.

Tom gently drew back the lift lever and depressed the power pedal. The diesel engine roared; the wrist-thick, all steel lifting cable tightened, stretched and slowly drew the turntable off the ground. Tom watched as the load shrank into the blue sky, then swung the boom to the left, over the tower.

Tom had been told that the turntable weighed 17,000 kilos, well within the crane's capacity. In fact, someone had apparently miscalculated: the turntable actually weighed 24,000 kilos. On top of the tower, five men peered up at the load, now hovering over them.

Tom was the first to know that something was wrong. He sensed the rear of his cab beginning to rise. With a groaning of metal, the boom was slowly pitching forward.

The men on the tower thought that the load was being lowered to them; in reality, it was falling. If it stayed on course, it would crush them and the tower. And the seventy-five-metre-long boom would slice through the adjacent buildings like a steel bar smashing teacups.

As the crane continued tilting, Tom felt the sickening sensation of being on a ship's stern, lifted by a giant wave. Every nerve in his body shouted 'Jump!' He tensed to leap through the cab door. But an image flashed before him: shattered buildings avalanching into the street – crushing pedestrians, flattening cars and buses, killing scores of people. He might, just might, be able to prevent the carnage. Could he live with himself if he didn't try?

On the ground, Tom's friend Roy Ledger, another crane-operator, stared in unbelieving horror.

'Oh, God' he thought, 'she's going over!' Yelling, workers round him began scattering. Up in the swiftly-tilting cab, Tom O'Brien made his decision. He refused to jump. Instinctively, Tom flicked levers and pedals, trying to swing the load out over the excavation. Hunched in concentration at his post, hands and feet moving like lightning over the controls, he felt himself being thrust high into the air as the screeching, groaning crane tottered on its front end, about to cartwheel. With vast relief, he saw the turntable crash into the excavation, exactly where he had hoped to place it. Then the boom and the cab, with its massive tractor treads, toppled into the pit. The thundering impact could be heard for blocks. People in the street ran in all directions, screaming in panic.

The only person hurt was Tom.

Themes: Courage, Cross, Easter, Encouragement, Jesus – his death, Love, Martydom, Persecution, Sacrifice, Suffering.

Scriptures: Psalm 27:14; Isaiah 53; Mark 10:45; Luke 10:27; Romans 3:21–25; John 11:50; 15:13; 1 Corinthians 13; Galatians 3:13; 1 Timothy 2:6; Hebrews 9:28; 1 Peter 2:24.

170: *Substitution*

Bob was driving a road-tanker through a town. It was a cold and wet night. He glanced in the rear-view mirror and saw flames. They were coming from the side of the tanker. He was carrying an explosive petrol-based chemical. Instead of stopping the truck, he put his foot down hard on the accelerator. He sped through the rain, with his hand on the horn until he was clear of the town. By then the cabin was full of flames. He swung the truck into a ditch and fell out. His face and hands and clothes were burning. When the police who were following came they wrapped him in a blanket to put out the flames. He was in shock and in awful pain. A thumb was missing and part of his jaw was gone and his windpipe was burned so that he could no longer breathe. But everyone else in the town was safe.

Themes: Courage, Cross, Easter, Encouragement, Jesus – his death, Love, Martyrdom, Persecution, Sacrifice, Suffering.

Scriptures: Psalm 27:14; Isaiah 53; Mark 10:45; Luke 10:27; Romans 3:21–25; John 11:50; 1 Corinthians 13; Galatians 3:13; 1 Timothy 2:6; Hebrews 9:28; 1 Peter 2:24.

171: *Substitution*

At one stage in India, the British were fighting a native monarch called Tippo Saib. In one of the battles several English officers were taken prisoner. Among them was one named Baird who had been severely wounded. One day, an Indian officer brought in fetters to be put on each of the prisoners. The wounded Baird was not exempt from the ordeal even though he was suffering from pain and weakness. A grey-haired officer said to the native official, 'You do not think you are putting chains upon that wounded young man?'

However, the Indian said, 'There are just as many pairs of fetters as there are prisoners and every pair must be worn.'

'Then,' said the officer, 'put two pairs on me. I will wear his as well as my own.'

Baird lived to regain his freedom. But the generous friend died in prison.

Themes: Courage, Cross, Easter, Encouragement, Jesus – his death, Love, Martyrdom, Persecution, Sacrifice, Suffering.

Scriptures: Psalm 27:14; Isaiah 53; Mark 10:45; Luke 10:27; Romans 3:21–25; John 11:50; 1 Corinthians 13; Galatians 3:13; 1 Timothy 2:6; Hebrews 9:28; 1 Peter 2:24.

172: Substitution

I was a prisoner during the war, and the treatment our captors meted out was diabolical. I had been very ill, and the food was poor. One day a crate of bananas was left where we could just reach them – it was a trap.

I was so hungry that I crept to where they were, and when no one was there I took one. Suddenly two guards pounced on me. I was dragged off to the commandant who ordered a public flogging as an example. The chaplain knew I would not survive the punishment and begged to take my place. Amused, the commandant agreed and ordered the whole camp to be assembled.

I was compelled to stand nearest the padre to witness the flogging. It was then that I began to understand what Peter meant when he wrote that Christ 'himself bore our sins in his own body on the tree'.

Themes: Courage, Cross, Easter, Encouragement, Jesus – his death, Love, Martyrdom, Persecution, Sacrifice, Suffering.

Scriptures: Psalm 27:14; Isaiah 53; Mark 10:45; Luke 10:27; Romans 3:21–25; John 11:50; 1 Corinthians 13; Galatians 3:13; 1 Timothy 2:6; Hebrews 9:28; 1 Peter 2:24.

173: Substitution

On 2 April 1987, two RAF crew men died when their F–111 crashed. The residents at Tenterfield in northern New South Wales believe that the airmen delayed ejecting to steer the plane to a deserted paddock. The men were hailed as heroes who were thought to deserve public recognition for their bravery.

The local newspaper editor said, 'There's a feeling among the townspeople that we owe a lot of lives to those two. It would have been no trouble for them to eject and not worry too much about where the plane was going to land, and who could have blamed them? But it looks like they stayed in the plane to guide it over the town.'

Themes: Courage, Cross, Easter, Encouragement, Jesus – his death, Love, Martyrdom, Persecution, Sacrifice, Suffering.

Scriptures: Psalm 27:14; Isaiah 53; Mark 10:45; Luke 10:27; Romans 3:21–25; John 11:50; 1 Corinthians 13; Galatians 3:13; 1 Timothy 2:6; Hebrews 9:28; 1 Peter 2:24.

174: *Suffering*

In his *Popular Account of Missionary Travels and Researches in South Africa*, David Livingstone tells of his encounter with a lion:

> It is well known that if one in a troop of lions is killed the remainder leave that part of the country. The next time, therefore, the herds were attacked, I went with the people to encourage them to rid themselves of the annoyance by destroying one of the marauders. We found the animals on a small hill covered with trees. The men formed round it in a circle, and gradually closed up as they advanced. Being below on the plain with a native schoolmaster named Mebalwe, I saw one of the lions sitting on a piece of rock within the ring. Mebalwe fired at him, and the ball hit the rock on which the animal was sitting. He bit at the spot struck, as a dog does at a stick or stone thrown at him; and then leaping away, broke through the circle and escaped unhurt. If the Bakatla had acted according to the custom of the country, they would have speared him in his attempt to get out, but they were afraid to attack him. When the circle was reformed, we saw two other lions in it; but dared not fire lest we should shoot some of the people. The beast burst through the line, and, as it was evident the men could not be prevailed on to face their foes, we bent our footsteps towards the village. In going round the end of the hill I saw a lion sitting on a piece of rock, about thirty yards off, with a little bush in front of him. I took a good aim at him through the bush, and fired both barrels into it. The men called out, 'He is shot, he is shot!' Others cried, 'He has been shot by another man too; let us go to him!' I saw the lion's tail erected in anger, and, turning to the people, said, 'Stop a little till I load again.' When in the act of ramming down the bullets I heard a shout, and, looking half round, I saw the lion in the act of springing upon me. He caught me by the shoulder, and we both came to the ground together. Growling horribly, he shook me as a terrier dog does a rat. It caused a sort of dreaminess, in which there was no sense of pain nor feeling of terror, though I was quite conscious of all that was happening. . . . As he had one paw on the back of my head, I

turned round to relieve myself of the weight, and saw his eyes directed to Mebalwe, who was aiming at him from a distance of ten or fifteen yards. His gun, which was a flint one, missfired in both barrels. The animal immediately left me to attack him, and bit his thigh. Another man, whose life I had saved after he had been tossed by a buffalo, attempted to spear the lion, upon which he turned from Mebalwe and seized this fresh foe by the shoulder. At that moment the bullets the beast had received took effect, and he fell down dead.

Themes: Missionaries, Obedience – cost, Sacrifice.

Scriptures: Matthew 10:1–15; 28:16–20; Mark 3:13–19; 6:7–13; Luke 10:1–20; Acts 27:27–28:6; 2 Corinthians 4:7–18; 6:4–10; 11:23–28.

175: Suffering

Joni was a great-looking blonde teenager. She enjoyed horse-riding and had a lovely family and plenty of friends. She had been a Christian for two years. But, as she traced her spiritual progress over this time, she realised that she had not come very far. She felt she was trapped in her emotional sins: anger, jealousy, resentment and possessiveness. She had drifted through her last years of school. Her grades began to drop and she began to quarrel with her parents.

So she became insistent with God, 'Lord, If you're really there, do something in my life that will change me and turn me around.... I'm sick of hypocrisy! I want you to work in my life for real.... Please do something in my life to turn me around!'

At last she wanted to be a fully-devoted follower of Jesus. A short time later, the storm broke in her life.

On 30 July 1967, Joni Eareckson dived into a shallow lake.

She was dragged out by her sister as quadriplegic. She became bitter and angry with God. She prayed – others prayed for healing – nothing happened. She knows that her accident was not sent from God. But she came to the point of trusting God in the storm of her life as she sought to follow him, especially in talking to others about him. Yet she is able to say, God is utterly dependable, no matter which direction our circumstances take us. And she says, 'I wouldn't change my life for anything. I even feel privileged.'

Themes: Anger, Bitterness, Healing, Jealousy, Possessions, Prayer – unanswered, Resentment.

Scriptures: Daniel 3:16–18; Matthew 5:22–24; 1 Corinthians 13; 2 Corinthians 11:30; 12:9; Philippians 4:13.

176: Suffering

Leonard Wilson was the Bishop of Birmingham in England. At his last ministers' conference he told of his experiences in a Japanese prison in Singapore. He was scared of being persecuted and prayed for courage.

On one occasion, four men were beating him repeatedly with rubber truncheons as he was under interrogation.

'Do you still believe in God,' they asked.

'Yes I do,' he was able to reply.

Then they asked, 'Why does God not save you?'

'God does save me,' he said feebly. And he went on to explain as best he could under the circumstances that by his Spirit God was helping him to bear his suffering. In fact, Leonard Wilson said God then gave him a vision to help him love those men.

Themes: Courage, Enemies – love of, Persecution, Suffering, Patience, Prayer – unanswered, Prisoners, Revenge, War.

Scriptures: Leviticus 19:18; Deuteronomy 32:35; Psalm 27:14; Proverbs 20:22; Daniel 3:16–18; Matthew 5:43–48; Luke 6:27–36; 10:27; 23:34; Acts 7:60; Romans 12:9–21; 1 Corinthians 13; 2 Corinthians 11:30; 12:9; Philippians 4:13; Hebrews 10:30, 36; 1 Peter 3:9.

177: Temptation

On the morning of Wednesday 10 April 1963, Lieutenant-Commander John W. Harvey, USA, took the nuclear submarine 'Thresher' to sea for post-refit trials. It was the beginning of a most tragic loss of life.

The tear-shaped vessel was 278 feet long with a beam of 31 feet, displacing 3,700 tons when it was on the surface. It cost $45 million. On board were a number of dockyard officials and firms' representatives, making a total of 129.

The shallow diving tests that day were successfully concluded. The next morning the submarine reported that she was starting a dive 270 miles west of Boston to her maximum operating or test depth – unofficially estimated at between 800 and 1,000 feet. The depth of water in this area is 8,400 feet.

At 7.52 am she had reached 400 feet and the dive was temporarily stopped for a few minutes for a routine inspection for leaks. At 8.09 am the 'Thresher' reported that she was at one half-test depth and from then on, for security reasons, all references to depth were reported in terms of test depth. At 8.34 am she was at test depth minus 300 feet and at 8.53 am was 'proceeding to test depth'.

At 9.12 am there was a routine communication check. A minute later a distorted message was received by James

Watson, the navigator on the Skylark submarine rescue vessel nearby. James heard the words: 'Experiencing minor problem. . . . have positive angle. . . . attempting to blow.' Then he heard a sound resembling pressure being blown into the ballast tanks. At 9.17 a final message reached Watson on the surface. He struggled to make out the words, 'Exceeding test depth.' Then there was a sound familiar to Watson; sounds of a vessel breaking up 'like a compartment collapsing: a muted dull thud.' The 'Thresher' had suddenly plunged towards the bottom at a very high speed. It had exceeded its crush limit and imploded.

Later, Admiral George W. Anderson, chief of naval operations, said. 'There would be no pouring in of water from ruptured points, no time to dog down (lock) watertight doors, no time for men to scramble to some point of maximum protection aboard. Only instant and complete collapse from all directions with the shock of an explosion.'

All that was left of the 'Thresher' was debris of twisted steel scattered over an area 1,000 by 4,000 yards.

However, in the trials of life, God will not take us beyond our depth or crush limit.

Themes: Endurance, Limits, Lord's Prayer, Risk, Testing, Tragedy, Trials.

Scriptures: Genesis 22:1; Exodus 16:4; 20:20; Deuteronomy 8:2, 16; 13:3; Judges 2:22; 2 Chronicles 32:31; Job 1:12; 2:6; Psalms 1; 66:10; 91; 118:5–6; 139:23–24; Isaiah 48:10; Matthew 26:41; Luke 8:22–25; 11:14; 21:9–19; 1 Corinthians 10:12–14; Philippians 4:8; 2 Timothy 2:3; James 4:7; 1 Peter 1:6–7; 2 Peter 2:9; 3:17.

178: Testimony – St Alban

In about the year AD 287, just north of what is now London, there lived a certain Alban. Though not a Christian, he gave hospitality to a Christian minister who was running from the Roman persecutors. Instructed little by little by his teaching about salvation, Alban gave up idolatry and became a wholehearted Christian.

After the minister had been staying with Alban for a few days, the Roman ruler heard that a Christian was hiding in Alban's house. He ordered his soldiers to make a thorough search for him there. When they came to the home, Alban immediately offered himself to the soldiers in place of his guest and teacher, having put on the long cloak the minister wore.

The judge ordered Alban to be dragged before the images of the devils in front of which he was standing and said, 'You have chosen to conceal a godless rebel rather than surrender him to my soldiers to prevent him from paying the well-deserved penalty for his blasphemy in despising the gods. You will have to take the punishment he has incurred if you attempt to forsake our worship and religion.'

The judge went on to ask him, 'What is your family and race?' Alban answered, 'My parents call me Alban and I shall ever adore and worship the true and living God who created all things.' The judge answered very angrily, 'If you wish to enjoy the happiness of everlasting life, you must sacrifice at once to the mighty gods.' Alban answered, 'The sacrifices which you offer to devils cannot help their devotees nor fulfil their desires and petitions. On the contrary, whoever offers sacrifices to these images will receive eternal punishment in hell as his reward.'

Incensed at this reply, the judge ordered Alban to be beaten. Though he was subjected to the most cruel tortures, Alban bore them patiently and even joyfully for the Lord's sake.

When the judge saw that he was not to be overcome by tortures nor turned from the Christian faith, he ordered him to be executed.

Legend has it that as Alban was being led to his execution he came to a rapid river. A great crowd had gathered. Alban, who desired martyrdom as soon as possible, came to the torrent and raised his eyes towards heaven. The river-bed dried up at that very spot, and provided a path for him to walk in. The executioner, who was to have put him to death, was among those who saw this. So moved was he that he hurried to meet Alban. The executioner threw away his sword and knelt down at Alban's feet, begging that he might be judged worthy to be put to death either with the martyr, or else in his place.

While there was hesitation among the other executioners, Alban went up the hill with the crowds and was executed. The solder who refused to behead Alban was also beheaded there.

Alban died on 22 June where St Alban's Cathedral now stands.

Themes: Courage, Enemies – love of, Persecution, Suffering, Patience, Prayer – unanswered, Prisoners, Revenge, War.

Scriptures: Leviticus 19:18; Deuteronomy 32:35; Psalm 27:14; Proverbs 20:22; Daniel 3:16–18; Matthew 5:43–48; Luke 6:27–36; 10:27; 23:34; Acts 7:60; Romans 12:9–21; 1 Corinthians 13; 2 Corinthians 11:30; 12:9; Philippians 4:13; Hebrews 10:30, 36; 1 Peter 3:9.

179: Testimony – Margaret Court

Margaret Court had an incredible tennis career in which she won a staggering sixty-six grand-slam titles.

When she started having heart palpitations, she went to her doctor. She discovered she had a torn heart valve. She was told she would be on tablets for the rest of her life. At the age of thirty-eight she faced a life sentence of medication.

Margaret met God when she was staying with a family in

the United States. She thought the wife was a religious nut. She kept giving Margaret Christian books to read. But, through her illness and this woman, Margaret met God.

Her personal life has been transformed. Interestingly, her heart got strangely better so that she no longer needs her tablets.

Themes: Conversion, Miracles, Prayer.

Scriptures: Matthew 8:5–13; 9:27–31; Mark 1:29–31, 40–44; 2:1–12; 3:1–6; 5:24–34; 7:31–37; 8:22–26; 10:46–52; Luke 13:10–17; 14:1–6; John 4:46–54; 9:1–34; James 5:14–15.

180: Testimony – Haslam

William Haslam was an Anglican vicar in Cornwall last century. He writes:

> I went into the pulpit and gave my text. . . . I do not remember all I said, but I felt a wonderful light and joy coming into my soul. . . . Whether it was something in my words, or my manner, or my look, I know not; but all of a sudden a local preacher, who happened to be in the congregation, stood up, and putting up his arms, shouted out in Cornish manner, 'The parson is converted! The parson is converted! Hallelujah!' and in another accent his voice was lost in the shouts and praises of three or four hundred of the congregation. Instead of rebuking this extraordinary 'brawling', as I should have done in a former time, I joined in the outburst of praises; and to make it more orderly, I gave out the Doxology – 'Praise God from whom all blessings flow' – and the people sang it with heart and voice, over and over again. My Churchmen were dismayed, and many of them fled precipitately from the place. Still the voice of praise went on, and was swelled

by numbers of passers-by, who came into the church, greatly surprised to hear and see what was going on. When this subsided, I found at least twenty people crying for mercy, whose voices had not been heard in the excitement and noise of thanksgiving. They all professed to find peace and joy in believing. Amongst this number there were three from my own house; and we returned home praising God.

Themes: Conversion, Evangelism, Joy, Praise.

Scriptures: Psalm 100; Luke 10:20; John 15:11; Acts 2:1–42; 9:1–19; 10:34–48; 1 Thessalonians 5:16–18; Hebrews 13:15.

181: Testimony – healing

Here is Suzetta's story which I asked her to write down for me.

When I was sixteen I had a very serious brain disease and spent several years in a wheelchair and later on crutches. I was not expected to survive, but much to the amazement of the medical profession I recovered, and apart from violent headaches, a slight unco-ordination and a continual sickness, I was able to enjoy life again as a 'normal' person.

I came to the London Healing Mission three weeks ago, and Tom prayed with me after the service.

It wasn't really until the next day that I appreciated what had happened. I hadn't had a headache. I hadn't been sick for a day. Even just twenty-four hours of peace was a miracle for me after five years! I was rather quiet at first about what had happened in case it was just a temporary thing. But as the days wear on I know it is really true. The joy, the freedom, and the real peace are inexplicable, wonderful. Jesus sure is alive!

Themes: Faith, Miracles, Prayer, Trust.

Scriptures: Psalm 37:3–5; Proverbs 3:5–6; Matthew 8:5–13; 9:27–31; Mark 1:29–31, 40-44; 2:1–12; 3:1–6; 5:24–34; 7:31–37; 8:22–26; 10:46–52; 11:22–24; Luke 7:1–10; 13:10–17; 14:1–6; John 4:46–54; 9:1–34; James 5:14–15.

182: Testimony – Wing-Commander Edward Howell

Wing-Commander Edward Howell was stationed on Crete when the Germans invaded and overran the island with bombs and paratroopers. Howell was badly wounded and taken prisoner. He spent many months in prison hospitals in Greece.

He discovered the real prison was not the stone walls around him but the stone walls within. What if there is a God, he thought? What if this God could set him free from being his own prisoner? He says:

> I decided to try. As I lay there in the darkness and despair of my prison cell, far from home, I gave myself and all I have to God – for better or for worse, for richer or for poorer, in sickness and in health, for ever. I entrusted him with my life, my possessions, my career and my family and friends. I committed myself to choose what was right to do and to be, from then on, in so far as I could honestly see it.
>
> At that moment of decision, God spoke to me. It was as though, by that simple act of will, I had switched on the light in a dark room. I saw the meaning of things for the first time. With an intense thrill, my mind told me, 'God is Love.' I began to see what that meant for me. My heart filled and overflowed. This was home at last, where you loved and were loved beyond all knowing. Nothing could ever separate me from it, so long as I chose to stay there. I was free at last, and no walls, or sentries, could take my freedom from me, so long as I chose to be free.
>
> I found myself praying, a thing I had not done for ten years

or more.... I was ecstatically happy and tears of joy flowed down my face.... I was sure and secure in the belief that now I knew the secret of living.

Themes: Conversion, Freedom, Joy, Praise.

Scriptures: Luke 10:20; John 8:31–36; 15:11; Acts 2:1–42; 9:1–19; 10:34–48.

183: Testimony – Jewess

At a conference on evangelism in the Philippines in 1989, Sue Perlman, a Jewess, told her story.

One day I met a stranger on a street-corner in New York City who shattered my misconceptions about the person of Christ. He was the first person really to communicate the gospel to me.... He told me that Jesus was not one of *many* paths to God but the *only* way, the *only one* who could forgive my sin....

I reacted in the customary Jewish fashion 'That's a very narrow-minded point of view,' I said.

He agreed with me and added, 'But it is true!' And something in me knew that I couldn't just dismiss Jesus.

I was invited to attend a church service.... Christians began praying for me from that night on, and my defences started crumbling. I didn't want it to be true that Jesus was the Messiah....

But.... I realised that to deny the truth would be senseless .... I, a Jew, embraced Jesus ... as my Lord and Saviour and, so, became a completed Jew, in the tradition of Peter, Paul and Priscilla!

Themes: Conversion, Evangelism, Forgiveness, Joy, Praise, Prayer, Witnessing.

Scriptures: Mark 11:25; Luke 10:20; John 14:6; 15:11; Acts 2:1–42; 9:1–19; 10:34–48.

184: Testimony – K.N. Nambudripad

K.N. Nambudripad is a surgeon, a Hindu by birth.

In 1959, he says, I was a resident in neurosurgery in Bristol, England. I was lonely and shy. My wife and four children were far away in India. One evening at a cocktail party I was sipping orange juice. A Christian nurse who was also drinking orange juice came to me. In the conversation that ensued she . . . . told me of Jesus Christ, her Saviour. I argued with her and told her my Hindu religion was good enough for me. However, when I went back to my room I began to think about Jesus. As a twelve-year-old boy I had heard of Jesus; I had read about him, and I had been greatly attracted to Jesus as a man.

I began to read the Bible.... I was greatly affected by the new reading of this book. I was affected by its authority. I said to myself, 'This is not at all like the Hindu books which I am used to. This sounds true. The writers have a real experience of God.' I said, 'John, who was a fisherman, had an experience of God which I, a Brahmin philosopher, did not have.' I said, 'I too must have this experience.'

It is now fifteen years since that encounter and surrender happened. Many trials and tribulations and difficulties have been my lot. I was put in a psychiatric clinic by my people. I was given electric shock, but the Lord was constantly with me. The Bible became my living friend and reality. I praise his name!

Now my wife and children, who had left me, are back with

me and they are Christians. Now depression has left me. I don't get depressed any longer. Jesus keeps me away from depression. I'm never lonely. Jesus is with me. When I operate, he helps me with wisdom and humility. When patients consult me with their tremendous problems, Jesus gives me compassion. Jesus has forgiven my sins; I have no guilt feelings; I can tell it to Jesus.

All the Hindu philosophy that I have learned is worthless when compared to the love of Jesus. I now get great joy in serving Jesus in [the] Christian Medical College and Hospital Ludhiana. And when I have free time, I witness in open-air meetings to the blessed love of Jesus Christ. He has delivered me. He has saved me.

Themes: Bible – authority, Conversion, Depression, Evangelism, Forgiveness, Guilt, Hinduism, Humility, Joy, Loneliness, Praise, Service, Wisdom.

Scriptures: Psalms 32; 34; 100; 121; Matthew 10:16–20; Mark 11:25; Luke 10:20; 18:9–14; John 14:6; 15:11; Acts 2:1–42; 9:1–19; 10:34–48; Philippians 2:3–11; 1 Thessalonians 5:16–18; 2 Timothy 3:16; Hebrews 13:5–6; James 1:5.

185: Testimony – Mrs Park

Mrs Park has a Methodist background. She was a congresswoman when the communist North Koreans attacked Seoul. As she was trying to flee south, she was captured and taken to an officer. After being questioned she was told she would be shot the next morning. In the meantime she was taken to a basement prison cell.

The next day, a young soldier of about twenty took her at

gun-point through the streets to where she was to be executed. She said, 'My eyes filled with tears as I began to remember all of the major events of my life.... I wondered if Jesus would forgive me and save me right then? Now with all the resolve I could muster I said, "Jesus, I am going to die in a few minutes. I have been a sinful woman. I don't deserve it, but please forgive this old woman her sins and save me like you did the thief on the cross."'

Then she said, 'Suddenly, I felt a joy fill my inner heart. . . . I was forgiven, I was free. I was ready to die.'

Despite her incredible circumstances, she began to sing aloud an old hymn she remembered. This was more than the young soldier could cope with.

'Shut up, old woman! Stop your singing now!' he shouted.

'Why should I obey you now?' she asked. 'Isn't it true that I am going to die anyway? I am now a Christian.... and I will take my last few minutes left on this earth to praise my Lord and Saviour.' She continued singing.

They came to a flat area in the city. The soldier took out a shovel and began to dig her grave. As he dug she sang. When he had finished digging he blindfolded Mrs Park.

He asked her, 'Old woman, do you have any last words you want to say before I kill you and bury your body?'

'Yes, I have only a few things to say. I have led a very wonderful life on this earth. But as we walked up here you had to notice that something happened to me. I woke this morning full of fear. Now I have peace and joy. You see, I was only a nominal Christian this morning, but now I am saved. I only wish that you too could know this wonderful Saviour Jesus Christ. May I spend the last moments of my life praying for your soul?' she asked.

She then stepped down into the hole that was to be her grave. She knelt and prayed. After just a few minutes she could hear the young soldier crying.

'You may shoot me now. I have finished praying,' she said.

But the young soldier told Mrs Park that he had a vision. He could not shoot her. He got down in the grave and released her and told her to run into the hills for safety.

Themes: Conversion, Evangelism, Freedom, Joy, Nominalism, Persecution, Praise, Prayer, Visions, Witnessing.

Scriptures: Psalm 100; Daniel 3:16–18; Mark 8:34–38; Luke 10:20; John 8:31–36; 15–11; Acts 2:1–42; 4:1–22; 6:8–8:3; 7:54–8:8; 9:1–19, 23–25; 10:34–48; 14:5–6, 19; 16:19–24; 21:30–36; 1 Corinthians 4:11–13; 13:3; 2 Corinthians 6:4–5; 11:23–28; 1 Thessalonians 2:9; 5:16–18; 2 Thessalonians 3:8; Hebrews 13:15.

186: Testimony – J.C. Penny

In 1929, the tycoon J.C. Penny's business was secure. But he had made some unwise personal commitments. He became so worried that he could not sleep. Then he developed 'shingles'. He was hospitalised and given sedatives, but got no relief and tossed all night. A combination of circumstances had broken him so completely, physically and mentally, that he was overwhelmed with fear of death. He wrote farewell letters to his wife and son, for he did not expect to live until morning.

In the morning he felt drawn to some singing he could hear coming from the chapel. A group was singing, 'God will take care of you.' There was a Bible reading and a prayer.

'Suddenly something happened,' he said. 'I can't explain it. I can only call it a miracle. I felt as if I had been instantly lifted out of the darkness of a dungeon into warm, brilliant sunlight. I felt as if I had been transported from hell to paradise. I felt the power of God as I had never felt it before.... I know that God with his love was there to help me. From that day to this, my life has been free from worry.'

Themes: Anxiety, Conversion, Evangelism, Joy, Praise, Stress, Worry.

Scriptures: Psalms 5: 46; 55:22; 100; Matthew 6:19–34; Luke 10:20; 12:22–31; John 15:11; Acts 2:1–42; 9:1–19; 10:34–48; Romans 12:12; Philippians 4:6; 1 Thessalonians 5:16–18; Hebrews 13:15; 1 Peter 5:6–7.

187: *Testimony – Little Richard*

Little Richard was the homosexual king of rock. He was the third of twelve children. He was black in a white society, gay in a straight one and crippled in a world where others walked tall. He had one leg shorter than the other, disproportionate eyes and a head too large for his body.

Cruelly, his father called him 'half son'. As a result he became a mama's boy with a flair for femininity and a mischievous streak.

His curiosity extended beyond music. Before he reached his teens he was having sex for money with a male friend of the family and masturbating ten times a day. He was nicknamed 'Richard the Watcher' because he enjoyed watching others having sex.

After he became a star, Little Richard's after-show orgies were hot stuff even by Hollywood standards. Soon he sank into drugged-out excess, supporting a $1,000-a-day cocaine habit. Yet, he says, he still read the Bible while breaking the commandments.

'There was a war going on in my body,' he said, 'a war between light and darkness.' Believe it or not he also said, 'I really wanted to be a Christian, but the devil took over till I finally decided that I had to be one or the other. . .'

That decision came after his brother died of a heart attack at the age of thirty-two. He realised it could be him. Then three friends died. So he allowed God's light to shine in his life. God's light in his life transformed him – not least his homosexuality.

Little Richard says, 'The habit [of homosexuality] is too deep for any human being to overcome without God. He gives me the strength not to want a man.'

Themes: Conversion, Evangelism, Homosexuality, Jesus – Light, Music industry, Conversion, Evangelism, Joy, Praise.

Scriptures: Leviticus 18:22; 20:13; 1 Kings 14:24; 15:12; 22:46; Psalms 55:22; 100; Matthew 6:25–34; Luke 10:20; 12:22–31; John 1:5; 3:19; 8:12; 9:5; 15:11; Acts 2:1–42; 9:1–19; 10:34–48; Romans 1:23–27; 12:12; 1 Corinthians 6:9; Philippians 4:6; 1 Thessalonians 5:16–18; Timothy 1:10; Hebrews 13:15.

188: Testimony – Bethan Ward

7 January. I went to see a specialist in Leicester today about a small lump on my neck. He suggested that it should be removed. I'm concerned about the timing as I am anxious not to miss too much of my ... course.

16 March. I received a very clinical letter this morning asking me to return to hospital for more tests. My mind ran riot. I desperately wanted to know more. I rang my GP and gently he told me what I had already feared – I had cancer.... After I put the phone down... I wanted to tell someone but I was on my own in the flat. I'll ring my mother, but how do I tell her? Somehow I found the words. Even over the phone I could

feel her acute shock – and I knew that Dad's reaction would be worse. Slowly during the day, however, for no apparent reason, the fear has been replaced by a deep peace. I don't understand but I find I can honestly say that I trust God in this.

20 April. At last I'm in hospital. All the waiting had become unbearable.

21 April. I got up early and took a bath. I lay there for quite a while, thinking and praying. As the time for my operation approached, I was scared but found great assurance in Isaiah 43:1–4. In the evening, just after I returned from theatre, I sensed my parents' concern and love as they held my hand even though I was barely conscious.

23 September. I saw my specialist today. He is very pleased with my progress.

31 December. Tonight marks the end of a rather special year for me ... but I am thankful ... thankful because God has provided me with all that I needed. Thankful because of the new perspectives I have gained, but above all I am thankful because in them God allowed me to see and know him as never before – that is very precious.

Themes: Cancer, Miracles, Prayer, Sickness.

Scriptures: Matthew 8:5–13; 9:27–31; Mark 1:29–31, 40–44; 2:1–12; 3:1–6; 5:24–34; 7:31–37; 8:22–26; 10:46–52; Luke 13:10–17; 14:1–6; John 4:46–54; 9:1–34; James 5:14–15.

189: Treasure

Nearly twenty years ago, Maurice Wright, a British farmer, bought a large painting from a neighbouring farmer for a couple of pounds and hung it in his barn.

After collecting cobwebs for several years, the painting was noticed by the farmer's accountant. Wondering what it might be worth, he took a colour photograph of it and sent the photo to Christies, the well-known London auction firm. Subsequently, he learned that the painting might be the work of Thomas Daniell, a highly-acclaimed nineteenth-century artist.

The painting turned out to be an 1808 Daniell. Art critics had been aware of its existence, but it had come to be known as the 'Lost Daniell', its whereabouts having been a mystery for over a century.

Wright sold the painting at an auction – for more than $90,000!

Themes: Gospel – its value, Kingdom of God.

Scriptures: Matthew 13:44–46; Mark 6:1–6; Luke 4:22–30; John 1:11–12; 2 Corinthians 4:7.

190: Unity

In France, during the Second World War, some soldiers carried the body of a friend to a local cemetery to be buried properly. However, they were stopped by the local priest.

The priest could see what was going to happen and so he said, 'Sorry, boys, you can't bury your friend here if he's not a Catholic.'

Although hurt and discouraged, the soldiers were not going to give up. They decided to give their friend their own burial service. They dug a grave and buried the body just outside the cemetery fence. Next morning, before they left the area, they went back to the grave to pay their last respects. The site was nowhere to be found. They looked for an hour combing the area. Then they went and found the priest asking him if he could help.

The priest explained, 'Well, the first part of the night I stayed awake, sorry for what I had told you. The second part of the night I spent moving the fence.'

Themes: Acceptance, Reconciliation, War.

Scriptures: Romans 14:19; 2 Corinthians 13:11; Ephesians 4:3; 1 Thessalonians 5:13; 2 Timothy 2:2; Hebrews 12:14; 1 Peter 3:11; 1 John 4:7–21.

191: Unity

I recently read about the reason why migrating geese fly in a 'V' formation. Each goose flapping its wings creates an upward lift for the geese that follow. When the geese do their part, the whole flock has a 71% greater flying range than if each bird were to fly alone.

Themes: Encouragement, Gifts of the Spirit, Loneliness.

Scriptures: Psalms 23; 121; 133:1; Matthew 10:16–20; Romans 12:3–8; 1 Corinthians 10:17; 12:12–26; Ephesians 1:22–23; 4:1–16; Hebrews 13:5–6.

192: Unity

A small child had wandered off in the tall jungle grass near an African village. The little one could not be found anywhere, even though the people searched for the rest of the day. The next day, the whole village turned out to hold hands with each other and walk through the grass together in a long line. The child was found, but he was dead – the cold night had been too much for him. In her anguish and through her tears the mother sobbed, 'If only we could have held hands sooner.'

Themes: Encouragement, Gifts of the Spirit, Loneliness.

Scriptures: Psalms 23; 121; 133:1; Matthew 10:16–20; Romans 12:3–8; 1 Corinthians 10:17; 12:12–26; Ephesians 1:22–23; 4:1–16; Hebrews 13:5–6.

193: Warfare

On 13 May 1940, Britain had been at war for eight months when Winston Churchill made his first speech in the House of Commons as Prime Minister.

> I would say to the House ... I have nothing to offer but blood, toil, tears and sweat.
>
> We have before us an ordeal of the most grievous kind. We have before us many, many long months of struggle and of suffering. You ask, what is our policy? I will say, It is to wage war, by sea, land and air, with all our might and with all the strength that God can give us: to wage war against a monstrous tyranny, never surpassed in the dark, lamentable catalogue of human crime. That is our policy. You ask, what is our aim? I can answer in one word: it is victory, victory at all costs, victory in spite of all terror, victory however long and hard the road may be.

A month later, on 18 June, Churchill made another famous speech in the House of Commons.

The whole fury and might of the enemy must very soon be turned on us.... Let us, therefore, brace ourselves to our duty and bear ourselves that ... for a thousand years men will say, 'This was their finest hour.'

Themes: Armour – God's, Enemies, Perseverance, Spiritual battle.

Scriptures: Romans 8:31–39; 1 Corinthians 9:24–27; 16:13; 2 Corinthians 10:1–6; Ephesians 6:10–20; 1 Timothy 1:18.

194: Wealth

John Wesley was a startling example of a Christian living in defiance of the materialistic trap. One of his frequently-repeated sermons was on Matthew 6:19–23 – 'Do not store up riches for yourselves here on earth.' John Wesley said that any Christian who takes for him or herself anything more than the plain necessities of life, lives in an open, habitual denial of the Lord. That person has gained riches and hell-fire!

Wesley lived what he preached. Sales of his books often earned him £1,400 annually, but he spent only £30 on himself. The rest he gave away. He always wore inexpensive clothes and ate simple food. He said, 'If I leave behind me ten pounds, you and all mankind bear witness against me that I lived and died a thief and a robber.'

Themes: Generosity, Giving, Greed, Lifestyle, Materialism, Money.

Scriptures: Psalm 112:9; Isaiah 55:10–11; Mark 10:17–31; 12:14–44; Luke 12:15–31; 19:1–10; 2 Corinthians 8 and 9; 1 Timothy 6:17–19; Hebrews 13:5.

195: Weddings

You will know that the central figure in any wedding is the mother of the bride. If it wasn't for her, weddings would be so simple – and so dull.

Once there was to be a wedding to beat all weddings. Mother was overcome with joy at the announcement of her daughter's engagement. Nobody knew it, but this lady had been waiting with a script for a production that would have met with Cecil B. DeMille's approval. The father of the bride began to pray for an elopement. His prayers were not to be answered.

Mother had seven months to work, and no detail was left to chance or human error. There were teas and parties and dinners. The bride and groom only met the minister a couple of times. Mother called weekly. The tuxedos were bought – not rented, mind you. If that was not enough, the engagement ring was returned to the jeweller for a larger stone, quietly subsidised by mother.

On the day, guests in formal attire packed the church. And the mighty mother coasted down the aisle with the grandeur of an opera star at a premier performance. Never did a mother take her seat with more satisfaction. She had done it. She glowed.

The music softened, and nine chiffon-clad bridesmaids stepped down the aisle while the groom and his men made the short march to their positions. Finally, the wedding march thundered from the eighteen–piece orchestra. The congregation rose and turned in anticipation.

The bride. She had been dressed for hours, if not days. No adrenaline was left in her body. Left alone in the adjoining reception hall while the march of the bridesmaids went on and on she had walked along the tables laden with gourmet goodies. She had absentmindedly sampled the little mints, the mixed nuts, the cheese and then the little sausages, and a couple of shrimps and then some pâté. To wash it all down and to calm her nerves she had a drink from the punch bowl.

What you noticed as the bride stood in the doorway was not the dress, but her face. It was white. What was coming down the aisle was a living grenade with the pin pulled out.

Just as she walked by mother, the bride threw up. And I don't mean a polite little ladylike 'urp' in her hanky. She puked. There is no nice word for it. She hosed the front of the church. She hit two bridesmaids, the groom, a ringbearer and the minister. Drained of everything, the bride went limp in her father's arms. The groom sat down on the floor too stunned to function. Mother fainted, slumping over like a rag doll.

Then, like a Marx Brothers fire drill, groomsmen rushed about heroically, flower girls squalled, bridesmaids sobbed, and those with weak stomachs headed for the doors.

Only two people were seen to smile. One was the mother of the groom. The other was the father of the bride. Eventually guests were invited to adjourn to the reception hall for drinks while a clean-up and restoration took place. Then the cast was reassembled and the deed was done without a hitch.

Themes: Humour, Marriage, Family relationships.

Scriptures: Deuteronomy 24:1–5; Matthew 5:27–29, 31–32; 19:3–12; Mark 10:2–13; 1 Corinthians 7:1–11.

196: Woman

A definition
Her symbol: WO
Atomic weight: 120 lbs.
Occurrences: Found wherever man is found, seldom in a free state.

Physical properties: Generally rounded in form. Boils at nothing and may freeze at any minute. Melts when treated properly. Very bitter if not used well.
Chemical properties: Very active. Possesses great affinity for gold, silver, platinum and precious stones. Violent reactions when left alone. Able to absorb great amounts of food. Turns green when placed beside a better-looking specimen. Ages rapidly without cosmetic attachments.
Uses: Highly ornamental. Useful as a tonic in the accelerating of low spirits, the most powerful income-reducing agent known to man.
Caution: Highly explosive when in inexperienced hands.

Themes: Family, Humour, Man, Marriage.

Scriptures: Proverbs 31; Ephesians 5:21–33; Colossians 3:18–4:1.

197: Works

A screaming nineteen-year-old woman trapped in a car dangling from a freeway in east Los Angeles was rescued in the early hours of the morning.

The woman had fallen asleep at the wheel of her car as she was driving home at 12.15 am. The car went through the guard rail and was left dangling by its left back wheel over the edge of an overpass. Every time the rescuers moved the car she would yell and scream. It took almost two-and-a-half hours for about twenty-five people – passersby, police, two truck drivers, firemen (as well as their equipment) – to secure the car and rescue the woman.

Later, Los Angeles County Fire Captain, Ross Marshall, said

something very interesting. 'It was kinda funny. She kept saying, "I'll do it myself".'

Themes: Grace, Law.

Scriptures: Acts 13:39; Romans 1:17; 3:20–4:25; Galatians 2:16; Ephesians 2:8–9; 2 Timothy 1:9.

198: Worship

Under the orange-and-blue striped canvas of the enormous marquee the sense of God's presence was giving rise to praise of a very enthusiastic nature. There were smiles everywhere, voices rang out, arms were raised, hands clapped and even some legs became liberated and danced for joy. In the midst of a group of worshippers sat a severely-disabled Christian man in a wheelchair. No one could have blamed him for feeling depressed or resentful of those around him who were praising God with agile and healthy bodies, while he could not even stand up. No one would have blamed him for excusing himself from the meeting and trundling off in his electric wheelchair out into the windy night and back to his room. Apparently nothing of the kind even entered his head, because as the spirit of praise grew stronger those nearby were treated to a lovely example of selfless praise. The wheelchair was well equipped for street use, and there he sat, flashing headlights, stop lights, indicator lights, warning lights, in fact anything that flashed, moved or made a sound was in use as he gave all he had in praise to the Lord he loved!

Themes: Dancing, Praise.

Scriptures: Exodus 15:20; 1 Samuel 18:6; 2 Samuel 6:14;

Psalm 100; Ecclesiastes 3:4; Mark 6:21–22; Luke 15:25; John 4:23–24; Acts 2:1–4; 1 Thessalonians 5:16–18; Hebrews 13:15.

199: Worship

In late 1993, Rod Denton, a South Australian Baptist minister, visited Argentina to see what he could learn from the revival sweeping that country. One of the places Rod and a team of thirty others visited was Olmos Prison in the city of La Plata, south east of Buenos Aires. The prison is a high-security, high density penal colony of over three thousand dangerous inmates from all over Argentina. Prisoners are housed in five-storey rundown squalid buildings with bars on the windows. There are arms and legs poking out of windows. Clothes and rugs hang down from the windows as well. As Rod was walking into this massive place he heard a noise in the distance. As he moved towards the sound it swelled to an incredible symphony of noise; a passionate sound, a strong beat that pierced the air. It sounded like a riot. The closer he got to a large old decrepit building the louder it got.

As Rod entered the building from the heat of the day, before him were eight hundred and forty prisoners praying and worshipping God in their chapel service. Revival had broken out. There is a colony of heaven in this hell. Over one thousand of the three thousand prisoners are now Christians. Once there were beatings and drugs and rape. Peace is starting to pervade the prison. Each night of the year, one hundred and twenty prisoners stay up in a vigil to fast and pray for the other prisoners. They tithe any income or gifts. They have a twenty-four-prayer chain seven days a week.

On this particular day, Rod moved among men worshipping

God with all their might. There was no overhead projector or books, just singing. The men were crying out to God and praising him with all the strength they had. They were lost in wonder, love and praise. In the worship there was an incessant clapping. The team of visitors nearly had to put their hands over their ears, the worship was so loud. Perspiration dripped from the prisoners. They did not want to stop. Many were prepared to stand for two hours because there were few chairs in the place. What chairs they had they gave to the visitors.

Rod sat in amazement. It was an awesome moment for him. He had never seen worship like this in all his life. He said he looked into the eyes of some of the prisoners and saw the very presence of Jesus in them.

Later in the meeting they asked for the privilege to pray for the visitors; that God would anoint them with the same Spirit that was in that place to take it back to their churches. The small group went and stood at the front. They were not prepared for what was to happen next. The eight hundred and forty prisoners prostrated themselves on the jail floor for fifteen minutes as they prayed. With tears running down their faces, they cried out to God for him to touch the visitors in a new way. Rod and the others felt the power of God come upon them. Many of the visitors fell to the floor with the power of God; this was not unusual. So powerful is the sense of God's presence in the worship that people walking along outside have fallen to the ground.

At the close of worship on this particular day, they embraced one another. A small man of about sixty, with a big smile and one tooth in the front of his mouth, went up to Rod. Rod wrapped his arms around him and prayed for him.

All too soon they had to leave. They got back into the bus in silence, not speaking for many minutes because they had seen something awesome they had never experienced before.

Themes: Freedom, Prayer, Prison, Singing.

Scriptures: Deuteronomy 6:1–4; Psalms 95; 96; 97; 98; 100; 122; 149; 150; Isaiah 6:1–4; Mark 12:30; John 4:20–24; 1 Corinthians 14:26–31; Philippians 3:3; Revelation 4; 5; 19:1–10.

200: X-Rated!

Barry Humphries, the actor best known as Dame Edna Everage, tells the following story from his university days.

The firm of H.J. Heinz had an excellent product called Russian Salad. It consisted largely of diced potato in mayonnaise with a few peas and carrot chips. Surreptitiously spilt and splashed in large quantities on the pavement of a city block, it closely resembled human vomit. It was a simple and delightful recreation of mine to approach a recent deposit of salad in the guise ... of a tramp. Disgusted pedestrians were already giving it a very wide berth, holding their breath and looking away with watering eyes. Not I, as I knelt beside one of the larger puddles, curdled and carrot-flecked. Drawing a spoon from my top pocket I devoured several mouthfuls, noticing out of the corner of my eye, and with some satisfaction, several people actually being sick at the spectacle. I have done this in many parts of the world and only in Fleet Street in the 1960s did I come close to being apprehended by a policeman. He, however, was too profoundly nauseated to take my name, and as he stood gagging on the salad-splattered pavement I made my escape.

Themes: Humour.

ACKNOWLEDGEMENTS

1) *The Medical Journal of Australia* (1984), 140: 681.
2) Susan Lindstrom, MSW, aged twenty-seven in Dr Magda Denes, 'Performing Abortions' *Commentary* (October 1976) pp 35, 37. From Melody Green, 'Children ... Things We Throw Away?' *The Last Days Magazine* (Americans Against Abortion, Box 70, Lindale, TX 75771–0070).
5) Adapted from Deborah Snyder, 'The Little Boy Who Couldn't Cry' *Reader's Digest* (June 1991) p 77–82.
7) William Barclay, *Ephesians* (The Saint Andrew Press: Edinburgh, 1958) pp 92–93.
9) Excerpt from Herbert V. Prochnow and Herbert V. Prochnow Jr., *The Toastmaster's Treasure Chest,* 2E, No. 2062, (HarperCollins 1988).
10) *The Advertiser* (Adelaide, 23 April 1988) p 7.
11) Adapted from *The Sower,* the magazine of The Bible Society in Australia (Canberra, Autumn 1991) p 6.
12) Adapted from Tom Rees, *Can Intelligent People Believe?* (Hodder and Stoughton: London 1971) pp 29–32.
13) Adapted from *The Sower,* the magazine of The Bible Society in Australia (Canberra, Summer 1991) p 12.
15) Stephen H. Travis, *Getting to Know the New Testament*

(Mowbray: London and Oxford, 1987) pp 1–2.
16) Roul Tunley, 'The Christmas that Stopped a War' *Readers Digest* (December 1983) pp 21–25. Adapted with the author's permission.
18) Adapted from 'Do We Know the Cost of Discipleship? *Go* Interserve: Box Hill, Victoria, June 1989) p 10. Used with permission from the publisher.
19) Adapted from Walter B. Knight, *Knight's Treasury of Illustrations (*William B. Eerdmans: Grand Rapids, MI, 1963) p 208.
20) Adapted from Bob Smalhout (Professor of anaestheiology, University Hospital Utrecht) 'What Killed Christ on the Cross' *The Sunday Times* (London 7 April 1985) p 13.
22) William Gowland, *Militant and Triumphant* (Epworth, London, 1957) p 26.
24) Adapted from Dick Innes, 'The Day that Changed the World' leaflet (ACTS: Norwood, South Australia; 1992). Used with permission from ACTS International.
26) *Newsweek* (2 August 1976) p 43.
28) John Pollock, *Moody: The Biography* (Moody Bible Institute of Chicago. Moody Press, 1983) pp 27, 39.
29) Deirdre Martin, 'Preaching to a Captive Audience' *Church of England Newspaper* (London, 12 June 1992) p 13.
30) Adapted from Billy Graham, 'The Evangelist and His Preaching: We Set Forth the Truth Plainly' in J.D. Douglas (ed.), *The Work of an Evangelist* (World Wide: Minneapolis, 1984) p 99.
32) Adapted with permission from Dr and Mrs Howard Taylor, *Biography of James Hudson Taylor* (Hodder and Stoughton, London: 1973) pp 239–41.
33) Adapted from Kenneth Surin, *Theology and the Problem of Evil* (Blackwell: Oxford 1986) p 116.
34) Adapted from Aquilla Webb, *1001 Illustrations for Pulpit and Platform* (New York and London, Harper and Brothers 1926) no. 123.
35) From Dick Innes, 'Lessons from Suffering, *Encounter*

(Norwood, South Australia, February 1988) p 14.
36) William P. Wilson, 'Hysteria and Demons, Depression and Oppression, Good and Evil' in John W. Montgomery (ed.) *Demon Possession* (Minneapolis: Bethel House, Minneapolis 1976) p 225–26. Reproduced with permission from Bethany House Publishers.
37) Loren Cunningham, *Daring to Live on the Edge: The Adventure of Faith and Finances* (YWAM: Seattle 1991) pp 68–69.
38) *Ibid.*
39) Adapted from Billy Kim, 'God at Work in Times of Persecution (Acts 7:54–8:8)' in J.D. Douglas (ed.) *Let the Earth Hear His Voice* (World Wide: Minneapolis, 1975) p 58.
40) David Watson, *I Believe in the Church* (Hodder and Stoughton: London, 1978) p 137.
41) Adapted from D.D. McNicholl, 'If at first you don't succeed....' in *The Weekend Australian* ('Weekend' 25–26 March 1989) p 16.
42) Adapted from Gary Smalley with John Trent, *Love is a Decision* (Dallas, Texas, and Milton Keynes, Word: Dallas, 1989) pp 189–190.
43) Adapted from Terry Lane, *As The Twig is Bent: The Childhood Recollections of Sixteen Prominent Australians* (Dove: Melbourne, 1979) pp 105–110.
44) Aquilla Webb, *op. cit.*, no. 161.
45) Ian Dunlop, *Palaces and Progresses of Elizabeth 1* (Jonathan Cape: London, 1962) p 27.
47) Adapted from Paul Y. Cho, *More Than Numbers* (Word: Milton Keynes, 1986) p 118.
48) Barry Humphries, *More Please; An Autobiography* (Viking: London, 1992) pp 126–127.
49) Adapted from *I'm Still Learning to Forgive* (Good News Publishers: Westchester, Ill).
50) Adapted from John Wimber, *Power Healing* (Hodder and Stoughton: London, 1986) p 86.
51) George Maronge, Jr., in *Leadership*, No. 12, 13 (1991)

p 49.
52) Adapted from Victor Hugo, *Les Misérables.*
53) Adapted from Aquilla Webb, *op. cit.* no. 946.
54) George Carey, *The Church in the Market Place* (Kingsway: Eastbourne, 1984).
55) Adapted from Michael Green, *To Corinth With Love* (Hodder and Stoughton: London, 1982) p 104.
56) Adapted from Jeffrey Pulver, *Paganini:The Romantic Virtuoso* (Herbert Joseph: London, 1936) pp 304–305.
57) Adapted from W. Henley, *Antonio Stradivari: Master Luthier Cremona, Italy, 1644–1737* (Amarti: Brighton 1961) p 62, and Paul E. Holdcroft) *Cyclopedia of Bible Illustrations,* (Abingdon Press, 1974) p 109.
59) Loren Cunningham, *op. cit.*, p 165.
62) Adapted from David Watson, *What Can We Know About God?* (Falcon/CPAS audio tape: London).
63) From Bruce Baskett, *The Advertiser Magazine* (Adelaide, 11 April 1987) p 11.
64) Adapted from John Young, *The Case Against Christ* (Hodder and Stoughton: London 1986) reprinted in *Church of England Newspaper* (London, 19 December 1986) p 9.
65) See William Paley, *Natural Theology: or, Evidence of the Existence and Attributes of the Deity* (John Fairburn, et al: *Edinburgh* 1822). Quotation from William Barclay, *The Plain Man Looks at the Apostles Creed* (Collins/Fontana: London and Glasgow, 1967) pp 27–28.
66) Adapted from Michael P. Green (ed.), *Illustrations for Biblical Preaching* (Baker Book House: Grand Rapids, 1989) no. 1406.
67) Adapted from *The Upper Room* (12 November 1983).
68) L.D. Weatherhead, *Prescription for Anxiety* (Hodder and Stoughton: London, 1956) p 120.
69) Lesslie Newbigin *Unfinished Agenda* (William B. Eerdmans: Grand Rapids MI, 1985) pp 63–64.
70) Adapted from 'Editorial', *Leadership*, 3 (no. 13, 1992) p 3.
71) Barry Kissell, *Walking on Water* (Hodder and Stoughton:

London, 1986) p 149.
73) Adapted from Michael P. Green, *op. cit.*, no. 889.
74) Adapted from *Group Movements of the Past and Experiments in Guidance* in J.I. Packer, *Knowing God* (Hodder and Stoughton: London, 1973) pp 213–214.
75) John Woolmer, *Growing to Salvation* (Triangle: London, 1983) p 84.
76) Adapted from 'Insights from Karachi', *East Asia Millions* no. 99 (1, 1991) p 4.
78) Edgar Allen Poe 'The Tell-Tale Heart' in Julian Symonds (ed.) *Edgar Allen Poe: Selected Tales* (Oxford University Press: Oxford 1980) pp 186–190.
79) Adapted from *The Advertiser* (Adelaide, 19 February 1992) p 17.
81) Adapted from *Leadership,* no. 5(2, 1984) p 44.
82) Taken from Francis MacNutt, *Healing* (Ave Maria Press: Notre Dame, IN, 1974) pp 193–194.
83) John Wimber, *op. cit.*, p 174.
84) *Ibid.*, p 145.
85) From C. Peter Wagner, *How to Have a Healing Ministry* (Monarch: Eastbourne, 1988) pp 104–105.
86) John Wimber in *Leadership*, no 612, (1985) p 127.
87) Adapted from Kate Semmerling with Andres Tapia, 'Haiti' *U Magazine* (February 1987) p 13 in C. Peter Wagner, *op. cit.*, pp 253–254.
88) Adapted from Teddy Saunders and Hugh Sansom, *David Watson: A Biography* (Hodder and Stoughton: London) pp 253–254.
89) Adapted from Tony Campolo, *It's Friday, But Sunday's Comin'* (Word: Berkhamsted, 1985) pp 76–82.
90) Adapted from Malcolm Muggeridge, *Conversion: A Spiritual Journey* (Collins/Fount: Glasgow, 1988) p 15.
91) Adapted from *F. Fernandez–Armesto, Columbus and the Conquest of the Impossible* (Weidenfeld and Nicolson: London 1974) pp 86–93.
92) Reprinted from John Koenig, *New Testament Hospitality*

(Fortress: Philadelphia, 1985) p 6–7.
93) James Dobson, *Hide or Seek* (Revell: Old Tappan, 1974) pp 9–10.
95) Adapted from Michael P. Green (ed.) *op. cit.*, no. 130.
96) Adapted from Richard Selzer, *Mortal Lessons: Notes on the Art of Surgery* (Chatto & Windus: London, 1981) pp 336–337.
97) Adapted from Kenneth Dodge, 'A Packaged Inheritance', *Parables, Etc.*, no. 12 (6 August 1992) p 1.
98) John Dunn, *Curiosity Collection* (Frederick Muller: London, 1982) p 61.
99) Len Evans 'Indulgence', *The Weekend Australian*; 'The Weekend Magazine', 7–8 September 1985) p 20.
100) Adapted from *The Advertiser* (Adelaide 30 April 1988) p 6.
101) Adapted from Kerry Redshaw, *The Bulletin* (Sydney, 21 January 1993) p 92.
103) Billy Graham, 'Loneliness', *Decision Magazine* (May 1972) p 8.
105) Michael Green, *Jesus Spells Freedom* (IVP: Leicester, 1972) p 80.
106) Adapted from Robert Fulghus, *It was on Fire When I Lay Down on It* (Grafton/Collins: London, 1990) p 181.
107) Michael Green, *op. cit.*, pp 81–82.
108) Barry Kissell *Walking on Water* (Hodder & Stoughton: London, 1986) p 77.
109) Adapted from Stuart Rintoul and John Lyons, 'Killer Who Said He Was Unworthy', *The Weekend Australian* (12–13 December 1987) p 8.
110) Barry Chant, *Marriage Joy Seminar* (Sydney, Seminar notes, 1993).
111) Adapted from Paul Tournier, *Marriage Difficulties* (SCM: London, 1967) p 57.
112) Barry Chant, *Straight Talk about Marriage* (Tabor: Unley Park, South Australia, 1983) pp 154–155.
113) Len Evans, 'Indulgence', *The Weekend Australian*,

'Weekend', (22–23 October 1988) p 18.
114) From Elizabeth Elliot, *Through Gates of Splendour* (Hodder and Stoughton: London, 1957).
115) *Leadership*, no. 6, (1, 1985) p 48.
116) Adapted from R. Demaus, *Hugh Latimer: A Biography* (Religious Tract Society, London, 1869) pp 520–524.
117) Betty Radice, *Pliny: Letters and Panegyricus*, 2 volumes (Heinemann: London; and Harvard University Press: Cambridge, MA, 1969) volume one, p 445 and Rick Gore, 'The Dead Do Tell Tales at Vesuvius', *National Geographic*, no. 156 (May, 1984) pp 557–613.
118) Adapted from Eddie Gibbs, *I Believe in Church Growth* (Hodder and Stoughton: London, 1981) p 358.
119) Based on a story by R.F. Holland, 'The Miraculous', *American Philosophical Quarterly*, no. 2 (1965) p 43.
120) Adapted from Dick Innes, 'Making Sense of Christmas' leaflet Norwood, South Australia, (ACTS: 1990).
121) Dr James Dobson, *The Strong-Willed Child: Birth Through Adolesence* (Tyndale House Publishers; Inc: Wheaton, 1978) pp 50–51.
123) Loren Cunningham, *Daring to Live on the Edge: The Adventure of Faith and Finances* (YWAM: Seattle, 1991) p 49.
129) Stephen Gaukroger and Mick Mercer, *Frogs in Cream* (Scripture Union: London, 1990) p 32.
130) Adapted from Walter B. Knight, *Knight's Treasury of Illustrations* (William B. Eerdmans: Grand Rapids, MI, 1963) p 133.
131) Adapted from Geir Kjetsaa, *Fyodor Dostoyevsky: A Writer's Life* (Macmillan: London 1987) pp 84–89.
132) Excerpt from Herbert V. Prochnow and Herbert V. Prochnow Jr, *op. cit.*, no. 390.
133) Simone Lang.
135) Billy Kim, 'God at Work in Times of Persecution (Acts 7:54–8:8)' in J.D. Douglas (ed.), *Let the Earth hear his Voice* (World Wide: Minneapolis, 1975) p 59.
136) Adapted from 'That's Life', *The Advertiser* (Adelaide, 15

April 1988) p 1.
138) Adapted from Alfred Stanway, *Prayer: A Personal Testimony* (Acorn: Canberra, 1991) p 25.
139) John Woolmer, *Growing up to Salvation* (Triangle: London, 1983) pp 112–113.
140) Adapted from Joyce Huggett, *Listening to God* (Hodder and Stoughton: London, 1986) p 64.
141) Used with the author's permission.
144) Adapted from Jeanette Grant-Thomson, *Jodie's Story: The Life of Jodie Cadman* (ANZEA: Homebush West, 1991).
145) Taken from Noel Becchetti, *Option Plays* (Zondervan, 1990).
146) Adapted from Don Richardson, *Peace Child* (Regal Books: Ventura, CA, 1974) pp 185–201.
147) Adapted from *The Advertiser* (Adelaide, 10 December 1992) p 3.
148) Lesslie Newbigin, *A Faith for this One World?* (SCM: London, 1961) pp 59–60.
150) Adapted from Paul E. Freed, *Towers to Eternity* (Thomas Nelson: Nashville, 1979) pp 190–191.
151) Adapted from Michael P. Green, *op. cit.,* no. 1155.
152) Adapted from Mrs Charles E. Cowman, *Harvest Secrets* (Olophant: London, 1956) pp 23–24.
153) Adapted from Douglas Webster, *Unchanging Mission* (Hodder and Stoughton: London, 1965) p 28.
154) John Woolmer, *Growing into Salvation* (Triangle: London, 1983) p 127.
155) Adapted from Aquilla Webb, *op. cit.,* no. 125.
161) Letha Dawson Scanzoni, *Sexuality* (Westminister: Philadelphia, 1984) p 46.
162) Adapted from H. Danby, *The Mishnah* (Oxford University Press: Oxford, 1933) p 252 ('Ketuboth' 5.6).
163) Jay E. Adams, *Competent to Counsel* (Baker Book House: Grand Rapids, MI, 1970) p 8.
164) William Barclay, *op. cit.*, p 67.
165) Adapted from Peter Hanson, *Stress for Success* (Pan:

London, 1989) p 73.
166) *Ibid.*, p 50.
167) *Ibid.*, p 55–56.
168) From Patricia Treece, *A Man for Others: Maximilian Kolbe Saint of Auschwitz in the Words of Those Who Knew Him* (Harper and Row: San Francisco, 1982; paperback edition 1994 RROW Franciscan, 1600 W. Park Ave, Libertyville, I1 60048, USA) pp 166–176; also Diana Dewar, *Saint of Auschwitz: The Story of Maksymilian Kolbe* (DLT: London, 1982) pp 110–113.
169) Adapted with permission from Richard Schneider, 'The Man Who Wouldn't Jump' *Reader's Digest* (November 1985) pp 132–140.
170) Adapted from B.J. Williams, *Spare Parts for People* (Wayland: Hove, 1978) pp 37–47.
171) Adapted from Aquilla Webb, *op. cit.*, no. 14.
172) *The Upper Room* (Friday 24 October 1980).
173) Adapted from Mark Ragg, 'Dead F–111 Crewmen Hailed as Heroes', *The Weekend Australian* (4–5 April 1987) p 5.
174) David Livingstone, *A Popular Account of Missionary Travels and Researches in South America* (John Murray: London 1873) pp 11–12.
175) Adapted from Joni Eareckson, *Joni* (Pickering and Inglis: London and Glasgow, 1976; with permission from HarperCollins Publishers Ltd).
176) Adapted from Tom Walker, *From Here to Heaven*, Hodder and Stoughton: London, 1987) p 161.
177) Adapted with permission from 'Debris Found in Atlantic: All Hope Gone for A–Sub' (Australian Press), *The Advertiser* (Adelaide, Saturday 13 April 1963) p 1; 'Inquiry On Lost Atomic Submarine: "Breaking Up" Sound Heard by Escort Ship', *Sydney Morning Herald* (Monday 15 April 1963) pp 1 and 3. Also see Commander Nicholas Whitstone, *The Submarine: The Ultimate Weapon* (Davis-Paynter, London, 1973) pp 47–50, 118–125; Drew Middleton, *Submarine: The Ultimate Weapon – Its Past, Present and Future* (Playboy:

Chicago, 1976) pp 178–185.
178) Adapted from Bede, trans. Leo Sherley-Price, *A History of the English Church and People*, (Penguin: Harmondsworth, 1955, revised 1968) pp 44–47. Bertram Colgrave and R.A.B. Mynors (eds.), *Bede's Ecclesiastical History of the English People* (Clarendon: Oxford, 1969) pp 29–35.
179) Adapted with permission from *New Idea* (11 April 1987) p 8 and (21 April 1990) p 22.
180) W. Haslam, *From Death into Life* (Morgan and Scott p 48, in David Watson, *One in the Spirit* (Hodder and Stoughton: London, 1973) pp 49–50.
182) Edward Howell, *Escape to Live* (Grosvenor: London, 1981), quotation from pp 93–94.
183) Sue Perlman, '"Uniqueness of Christ" Testimony' in J.D. Douglas (ed.), *Proclaim Christ Until He Comes* (World Wide: Minneapolis, 1990) pp 312–313.
184) K.N. Nambudripad 'Testimony' in J.D. Douglas (ed.), *op. cit.*, p 413.
185) Adapted from Paul Y. Cho, *More Than Numbers* (Word: Milton Keynes 1986) pp 73–76.
186) Adapted from Dale Carnegie, *How to Stop Worrying and Start Living* (Simon and Schuster: New York, 1948) pp 253–254.
187) Adapted from Vicky Jo Radovsky, 'Little Richard: How Rock's Gay Legend Switched on to God' *The Weekend Australian* (8–9 December 1984) p 7.
188) Adapted from 'Look Back in Wonder' *All Souls Magazine* (January – February 1983) p 7.
190) Adapted from John MacArthur, *The Church: The Body of Christ* (Zondervan: Grand Rapids, MI, 1973) p 22, with permission from 'Grace to You', P.O. Box 4000, Panorama City, CA 91412, USA.
192) Adapted from Michael P. Green *op. cit.*, no. 201
194) Adapted from Ronald J. Sider, *Rich Christians in an Age of Hunger* (Hodder and Stoughton: London, 1977) p 150, and Word Publishing, Dallas, Texas. All rights reserved.
195) Adapted from Robert Fulghum, *It was on Fire When I*

Lay Down on It (Grafton/Collins: London, 1990) chapter one.
196) From Barry Chant, *Straight Talk about Marriage* (Tabor: Unley Park, South Australia, 1983) p 20.
197) From *Los Angeles Times,* Part II, (20 November 1988) pp 1–2.
198) Graham Kendrick *Worship*, (Kingsway, Eastbourne, 1984) p 99.
199) Used with permission.
200) Barry Humphries, *More Please* (Viking: London, 1992) p 118

BIBLICAL PASSAGES

John

NAMES, PLACES AND THEMES